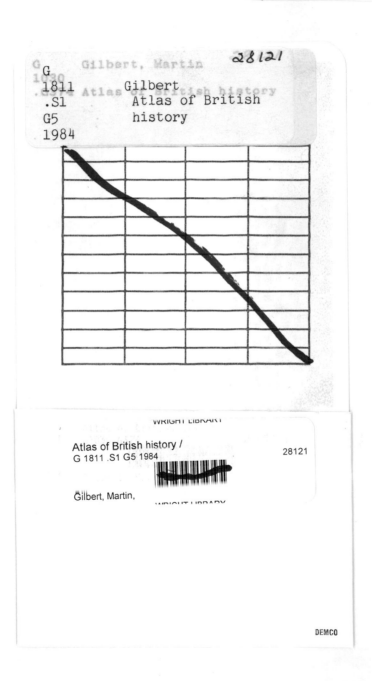

ATLAS OF
BRITISH HISTORY

ATLAS OF
BRITISH HISTORY

MARTIN GILBERT

Fellow of Merton College, Oxford

Cartography by ARTHUR BANKS

DORSET PRESS

Library of Congress Catalog Card Number: 69-17101

1984 Dorset Press

This edition published by Dorset Press, a division of MARBORO BOOKS Corp., by arrangement with the proprietor.
Originally published as *British History Atlas*.

British History Atlas was first published in Great Britain in 1968 by Weidenfeld and Nicolson, London

ISBN 0-88029-017-X

Printed in the United States of America

Preface

The maps in this atlas are intended to provide a visual introduction to British history. I have used the word 'British' in its widest scope, including when relevant England, Scotland, Ireland and Wales, the changing overseas empire, the wars and treaties in which Britain engaged, the alliances in time of peace, the growth of industry and trade, and, on five of the maps, famine and plague.

The story of the British Isles forms the central theme. I have included maps to illustrate economic, social and political problems as well as territorial and military ones. I hope this atlas will help to show that there is more to British history than Hastings and Crécy, Blenheim and Waterloo, Passchendaele and Dunkirk, all of which moments of glory I have tried to put in their wider, and no less important, contexts.

For the maps covering the period before the Norman Conquest the sources are often conflicting on specific details. I have therefore drawn these maps on the basis of probability. In many instances precise knowledge of early frontiers is lacking. I have tried nevertheless to give a clear if also, of necessity, an approximate picture.

As British history advances from wattle huts to timber mansions, and thence on to steel and concrete, so too do the number and variety of facts available to the historian. This is reflected in the maps themselves. I have tried to avoid too complex or too cluttered a page; but a map cannot always satisfy all the demands made upon it, and only the reader can judge where clarity of design and sufficiency of information have been successfully combined.

I am under an obligation of gratitude to those historians and colleagues who kindly scrutinised my draft maps at an early stage, and who made many suggestions for their scope and improvement; in particular Dr J. M. Wallace-Hadrill, Dr Roger Highfield, Mr Ralph Davis, Mr T. F. R. G. Braun, Dr C. C. Davies and Miss Barbara Malament. When the maps were more completed, they were checked by Mr Adrian Scheps, Mr Edmund Ranallo, Mrs Elizabeth Goold, Mr Tony Lawdham and Mrs Jean Kelly, to all of whom my thanks are due.

Both the publishers and I are beholden to the cartographic skill and energy of Mr Arthur Banks, who transformed rough drafts, pencil sketches and complex instructions into maps of the highest clarity and most attractive design.

I should greatly welcome any corrections of these maps for future editions.

MARTIN GILBERT
Merton College, Oxford

1968

List of Maps

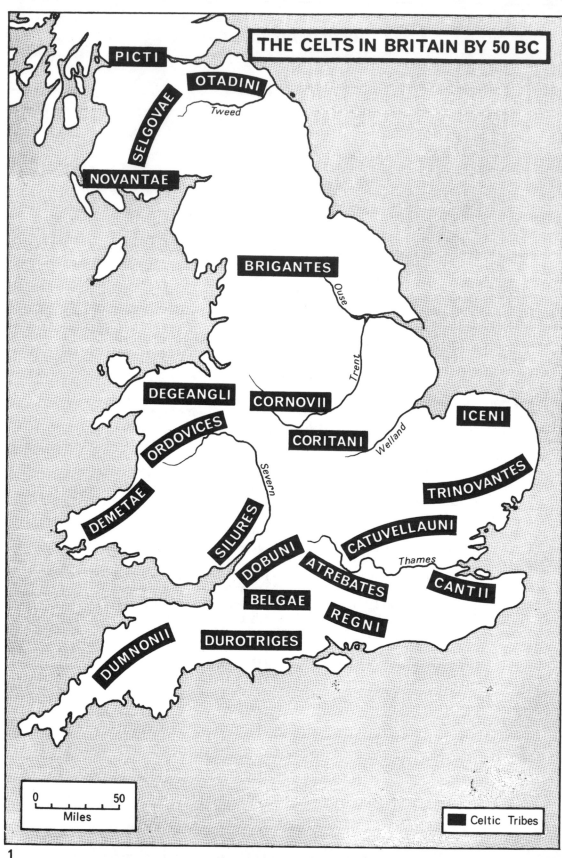

THE CELTS IN BRITAIN BY 50 BC

PICTI

OTADINI

SELGOVAE

Tweed

NOVANTAE

BRIGANTES

Ouse

Trent

DEGEANGLI

CORNOVII

ICENI

ORDOVICES

CORITANI

Welland

DEMETAE

Severn

TRINOVANTES

SILURES

CATUVELLAUNI

DOBUNI

ATREBATES

Thames

CANTII

BELGAE

REGNI

DUMNONII

DUROTRIGES

0   50
Miles

■ Celtic Tribes

1

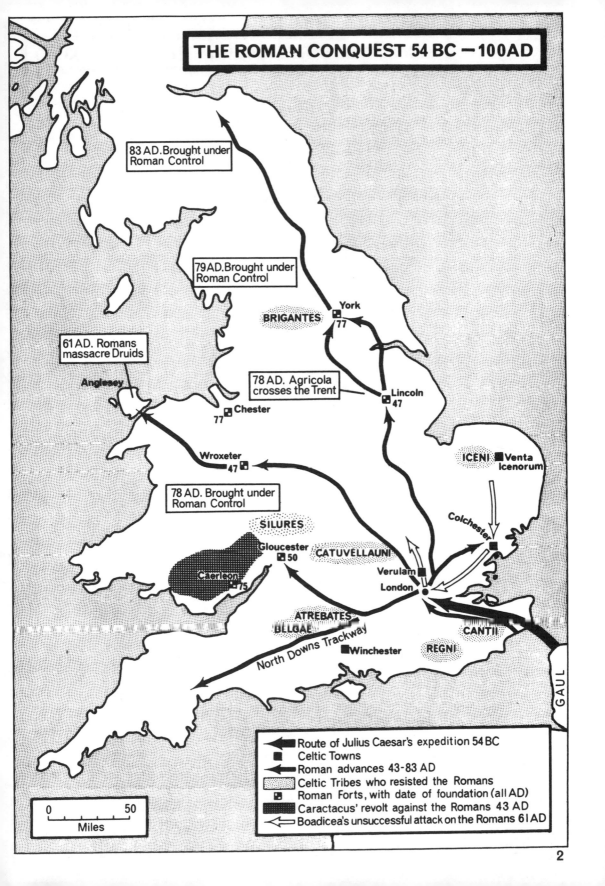

THE ROMAN CONQUEST 54 BC — 100AD

83 AD. Brought under Roman Control

79 AD. Brought under Roman Control

61 AD. Romans massacre Druids

78 AD. Agricola crosses the Trent

78 AD. Brought under Roman Control

BRIGANTES

York
77

Anglesey

Chester
77

Lincoln
47

Wroxeter
47

ICENI · Venta Icenorum

SILURES

Gloucester
50

CATUVELLAUNI

Colchester

Caerleon
75

Verulam

London

ATREBATES

BELGAE

Winchester

North Downs Trackway

CANTII

REGNI

GAUL

Miles
0   50

Route of Julius Caesar's expedition 54 BC
Celtic Towns
Roman advances 43-83 AD
Celtic Tribes who resisted the Romans
Roman Forts, with date of foundation (all AD)
Caractacus' revolt against the Romans 43 AD
Boadicea's unsuccessful attack on the Romans 61 AD

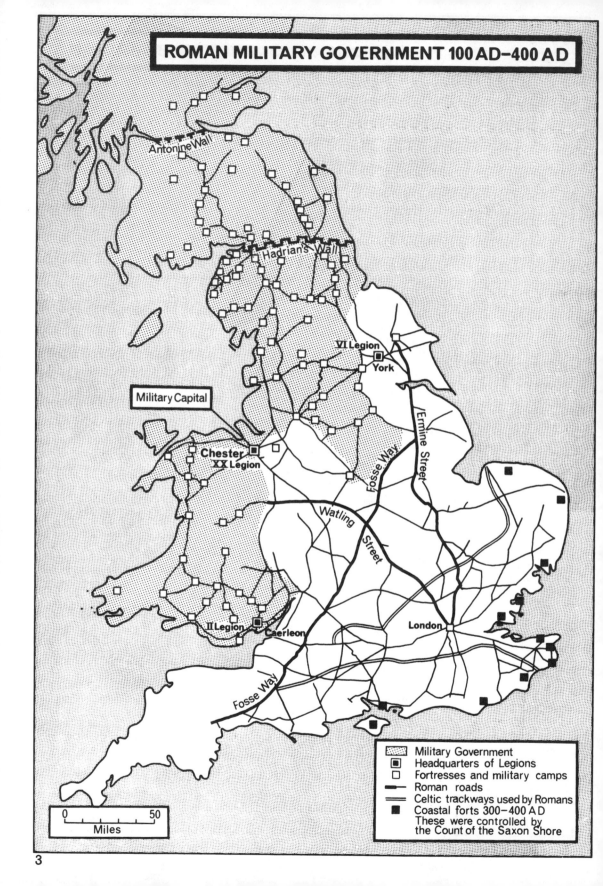

ROMAN MILITARY GOVERNMENT 100 AD–400 AD

Antonine Wall

Hadrian's Wall

VI Legion
York

Military Capital

Chester
XX Legion

Ermine Street

Fosse Way

Watling Street

II Legion
Caerleon

London

Fosse Way

Military Government
Headquarters of Legions
Fortresses and military camps
Roman roads
Celtic trackways used by Romans
Coastal forts 300–400 A D
These were controlled by
the Count of the Saxon Shore

0   50
Miles

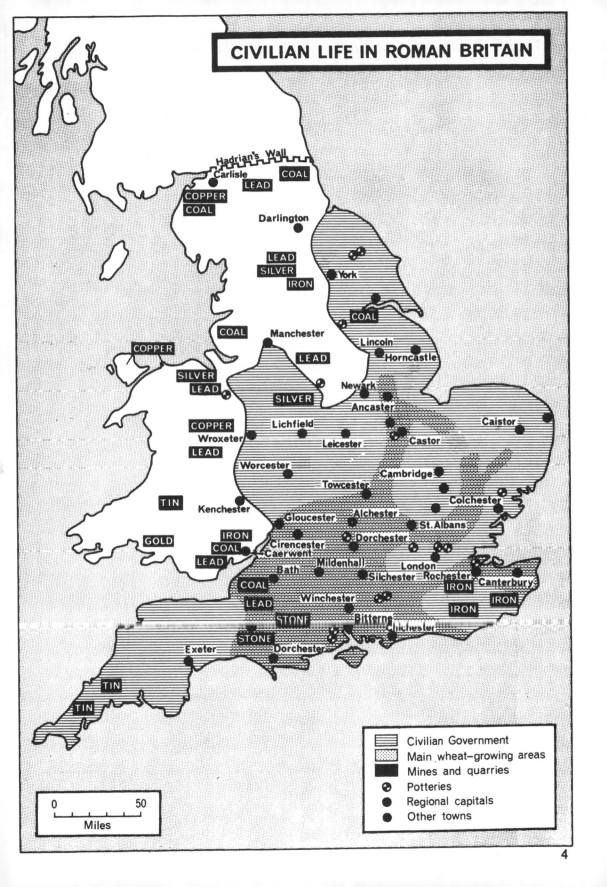

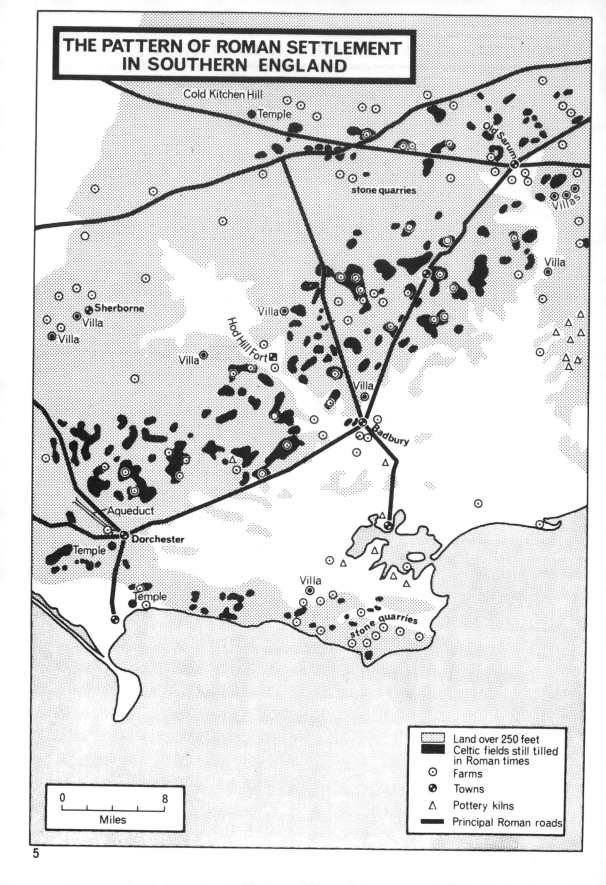

THE PATTERN OF ROMAN SETTLEMENT IN SOUTHERN ENGLAND

Cold Kitchen Hill

● Temple

Old Sarum

stone quarries

Villas

Villa

Sherborne
● Villa
● Villa

Villa

Hod Hill Fort

Villa

Villa

Badbury

Villa

Aqueduct

Dorchester

Temple

Temple

Villa

stone quarries

	Land over 250 feet
	Celtic fields still tilled in Roman times
⊙	Farms
⊕	Towns
△	Pottery kilns
▬	Principal Roman roads

0   8
Miles

5

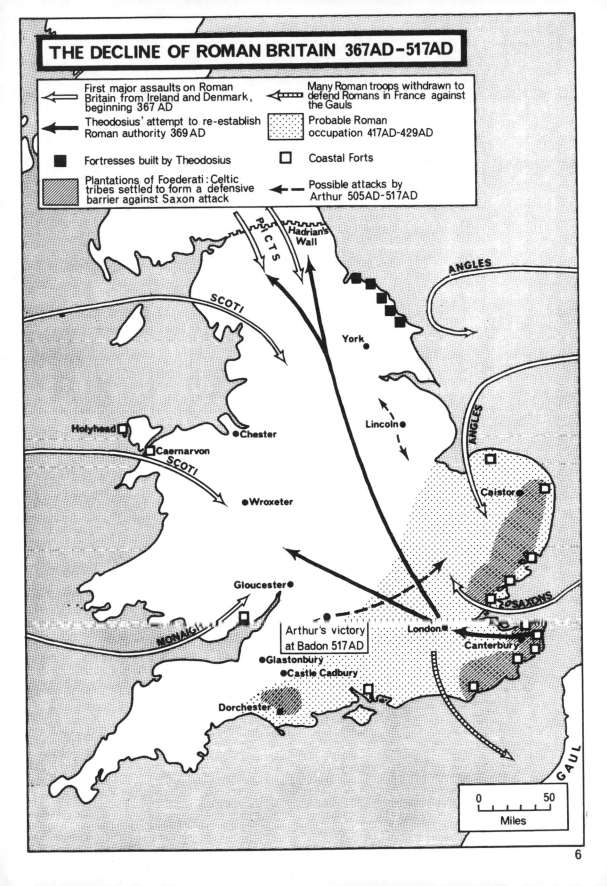

THE DECLINE OF ROMAN BRITAIN 367AD–517AD

← First major assaults on Roman Britain from Ireland and Denmark, beginning 367 AD

← Theodosius' attempt to re-establish Roman authority 369 AD

■ Fortresses built by Theodosius

▨ Plantations of Foederati: Celtic tribes settled to form a defensive barrier against Saxon attack

←┅ Many Roman troops withdrawn to defend Romans in France against the Gauls

⬚ Probable Roman occupation 417AD–429AD

□ Coastal Forts

←-- Possible attacks by Arthur 505AD–517AD

PICTS

Hadrian's Wall

ANGLES

SCOTI

York

ANGLES

Holyhead

Chester

Lincoln

Caernarvon

SCOTI

Caistor

Wroxeter

Gloucester

SAXONS

London

Canterbury

Arthur's victory at Badon 517AD

Glastonbury

Castle Cadbury

Dorchester

GAUL

0   50
Miles

6

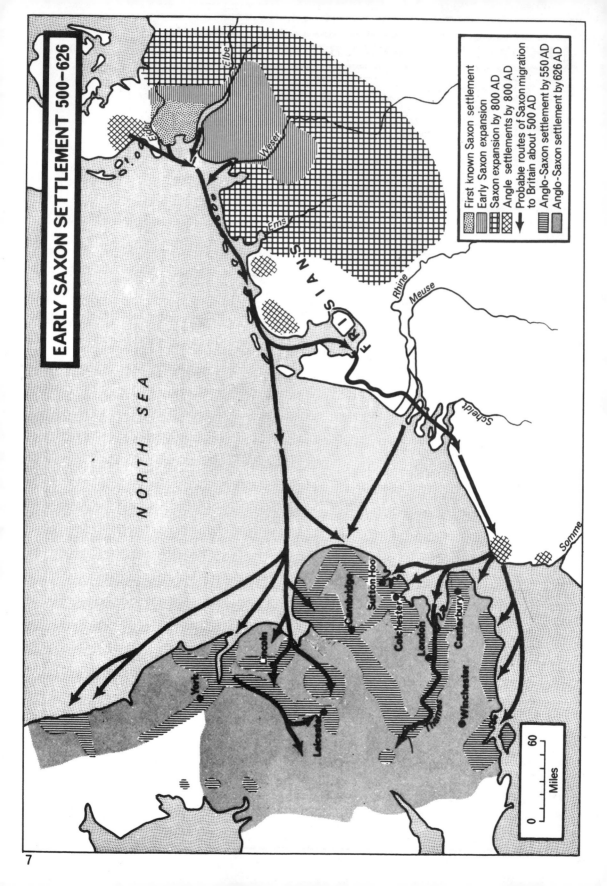

EARLY SAXON SETTLEMENT 500–626

Legend:
- First known Saxon settlement
- Early Saxon expansion
- Saxon expansion by 800 AD
- Angle settlements by 800 AD
- Probable routes of Saxon migration to Britain about 500 AD
- Anglo-Saxon settlement by 550 AD
- Anglo-Saxon settlement by 626 AD

NORTH SEA

FRISIANS

Elbe
Weser
Ems
Rhine
Meuse
Scheldt
Somme

York
Lincoln
Lichfield
Cambridge
Sutton Hoo
Colchester
London
Canterbury
Winchester
Thames

0   60
Miles

SAXON KINGDOMS AND BRETWALDASHIPS 630-829

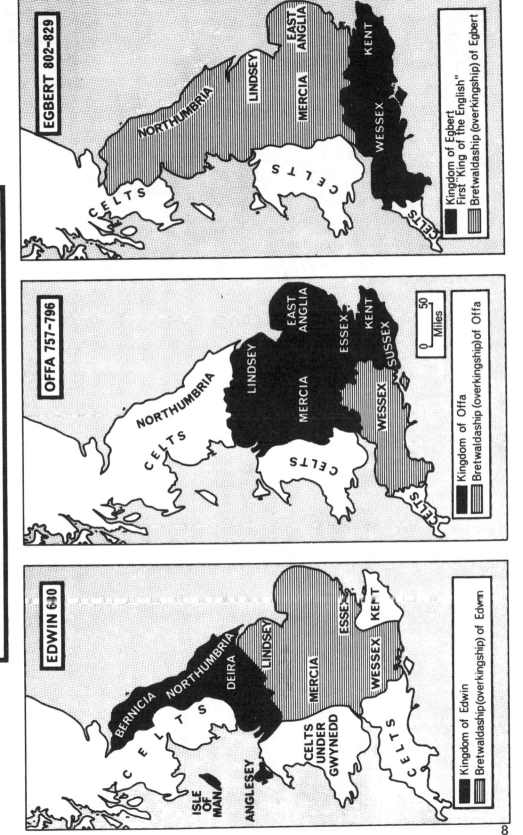

EGBERT 802-829

NORTHUMBRIA
LINDSEY
EAST ANGLIA
MERCIA
KENT
WESSEX
CELTS
CELTS

■ Kingdom of Egbert
First "King of the English"
▥ Bretwaldaship (overkingship) of Egbert

OFFA 757-796

NORTHUMBRIA
CELTS
LINDSEY
EAST ANGLIA
MERCIA
ESSEX
KENT
WESSEX
SUSSEX
CELTS
CELTS

0   50
Miles

■ Kingdom of Offa
▥ Bretwaldaship (overkingship) of Offa

EDWIN 630

BERNICIA
NORTHUMBRIA
DEIRA
CELTS
LINDSEY
MERCIA
ESSEX
WESSEX
KENT
CELTS UNDER GWYNEDD
ISLE OF MAN
ANGLESEY
CELTS

■ Kingdom of Edwin
▥ Bretwaldaship (overkingship) of Edwin

8

THE CHURCH 700-850

† Abercorn
Coldingham
Lindisfarne
† Melrose

L I N D I S F A R N E

WHITHORN

ⱡ Coquet Island

† Tynemouth
Hexham † † Jarrow
Monkwearmouth

† Whithorn

HEXHAM

Hartlepool
†Gainford
Gilling
Sockburn Whitby
Lastingham Hackness†
†Ripon
York

† Barrow
Syddensis Civitas
(site not known)

LINDSEY

LICHFIELD

Repton † Breedon
Lichfield
Peterborough †
Leicester †Oundle Ely
† Brixworth
LEICESTER

Elmham
ELMHAM

Dunwich
† Bury St.
Edmunds
DUNWICH

HEREFORD

Worcester
Hereford

WORCESTER

DORCHESTER

LONDON

† Malmesbury
Abingdon Dorchester
Barking
London

ROCH-
ESTER
Minster
CANTER-
BURY
Dover
Folkestone
Lyminge

WINCHESTER
Woking

Glastonbury †
Sherborne
†Tisbury
Nursling †
Winchester

SELSEY
Selsey

SHERBORNE
Exeter †
Wimborne †

†	Religious houses founded by 850
⊕	Double houses where monks and nuns lived under the rule of an abbess
—	Approximate diocesan boundaries
●	Diocesan seats
▨	Archbishoprics

0   50
Miles

9

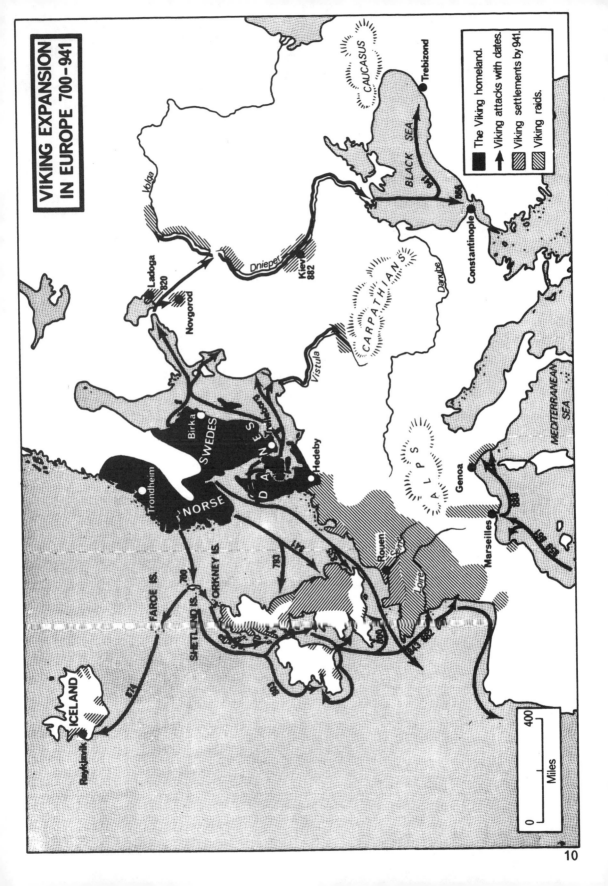

VIKING EXPANSION
IN EUROPE 700–941

The Viking homeland.
→ Viking attacks with dates.
Viking settlements by 941.
Viking raids.

BLACK SEA
Trebizond
Constantinople
CAUCASUS
CARPATHIANS
Danube
Dniepet
Kiev 882
Vistula
Volga
Ladoga 920
Novgorod
SWEDES
Birka
NORSE
Trondheim
DANES
Hedeby
ALPS
Genoa
Marseilles
MEDITERRANEAN SEA
Rouen
FAROE IS. 700
SHETLAND IS.
ORKNEY IS.
793
ICELAND
Reykjavik

0   400
Miles

10

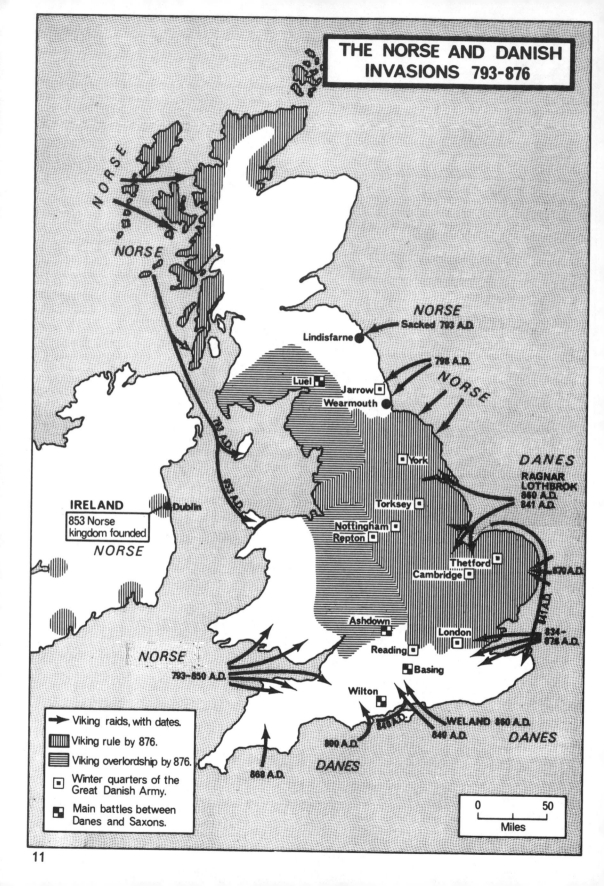

THE NORSE AND DANISH INVASIONS 793-876

NORSE

NORSE

NORSE

NORSE
Sacked 793 A.D.

Lindisfarne

796 A.D.

NORSE

Luel
Jarrow
Wearmouth

DANES
RAGNAR
LOTHBROK
860 A.D.
841 A.D.

York

IRELAND
853 Norse
kingdom founded

Dublin

NORSE

Torksey

Nottingham
Repton

Thetford

Cambridge

Ashdown

London

Reading

Basing

NORSE

793-850 A.D.

Wilton

WELAND 860 A.D.
840 A.D.

DANES

860 A.D.

DANES

869 A.D.

→ Viking raids, with dates.

▨ Viking rule by 876.

▤ Viking overlordship by 876.

☐ Winter quarters of the
Great Danish Army.

☐ Main battles between
Danes and Saxons.

0   50

Miles

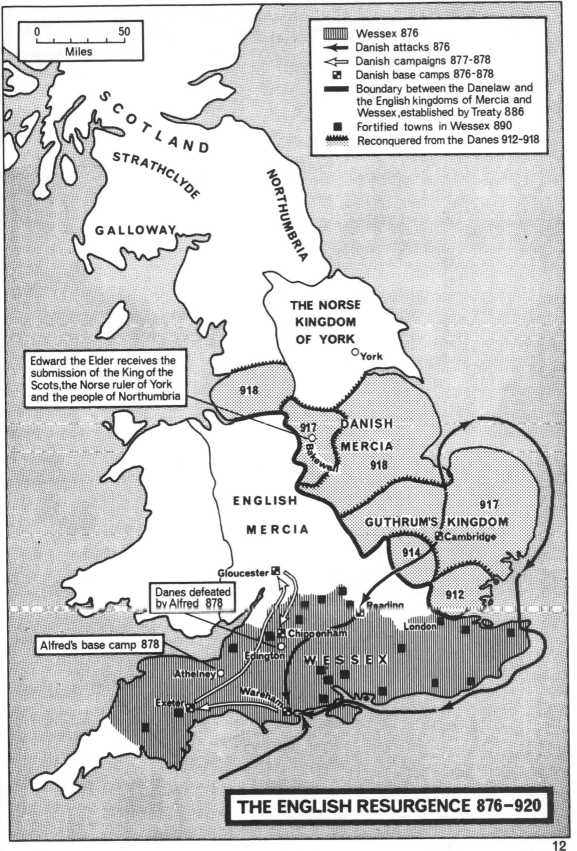

Scale: 0 — 50 Miles

Legend:
- Wessex 876
- Danish attacks 876
- Danish campaigns 877-878
- Danish base camps 876-878
- Boundary between the Danelaw and the English kingdoms of Mercia and Wessex, established by Treaty 886
- Fortified towns in Wessex 890
- Reconquered from the Danes 912-918

SCOTLAND

STRATHCLYDE

GALLOWAY

NORTHUMBRIA

THE NORSE KINGDOM OF YORK

○York

Edward the Elder receives the submission of the King of the Scots, the Norse ruler of York and the people of Northumbria

918

917
○Bakewell

DANISH MERCIA

918

ENGLISH MERCIA

GUTHRUM'S KINGDOM

917

□Cambridge

914

912

Gloucester□

Danes defeated by Alfred 878

Reading□

London□

Alfred's base camp 878

Chippenham

Edington

WESSEX

Athelney○

Exeter□

Wareham□

Way

THE ENGLISH RESURGENCE 876–920

12

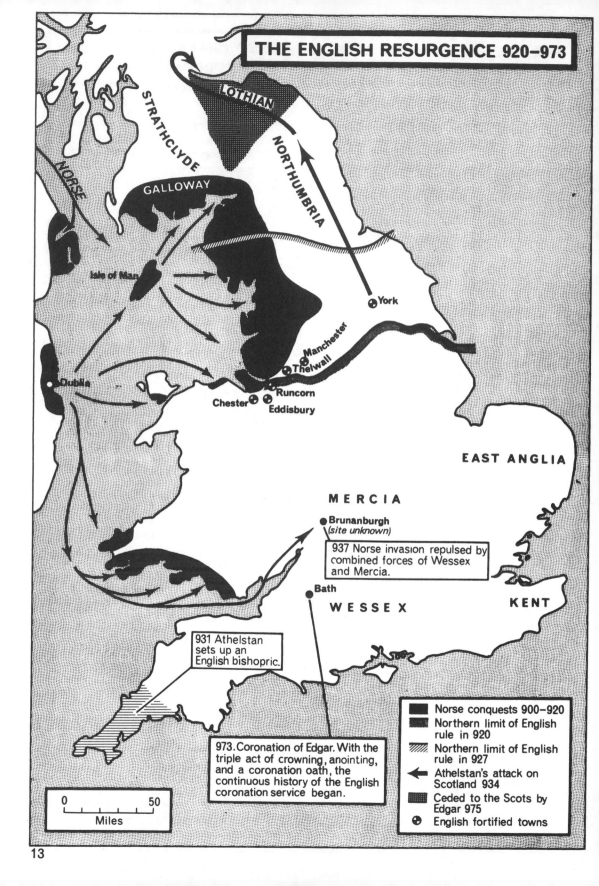

THE ENGLISH RESURGENCE 920–973

STRATHCLYDE

LOTHIAN

NORTHUMBRIA

NORSE

GALLOWAY

Isle of Man

Dublin

York

Manchester
Thelwall

Runcorn
Chester ⊕ ⊕
Eddisbury

EAST ANGLIA

MERCIA

● Brunanburgh
(site unknown)

937 Norse invasion repulsed by
combined forces of Wessex
and Mercia.

● Bath

WESSEX

KENT

931 Athelstan
sets up an
English bishopric.

973. Coronation of Edgar. With the
triple act of crowning, anointing,
and a coronation oath, the
continuous history of the English
coronation service began.

0   50
Miles

■ Norse conquests 900–920
■ Northern limit of English
rule in 920
▨ Northern limit of English
rule in 927
← Athelstan's attack on
Scotland 934
▦ Ceded to the Scots by
Edgar 975
⊕ English fortified towns

13

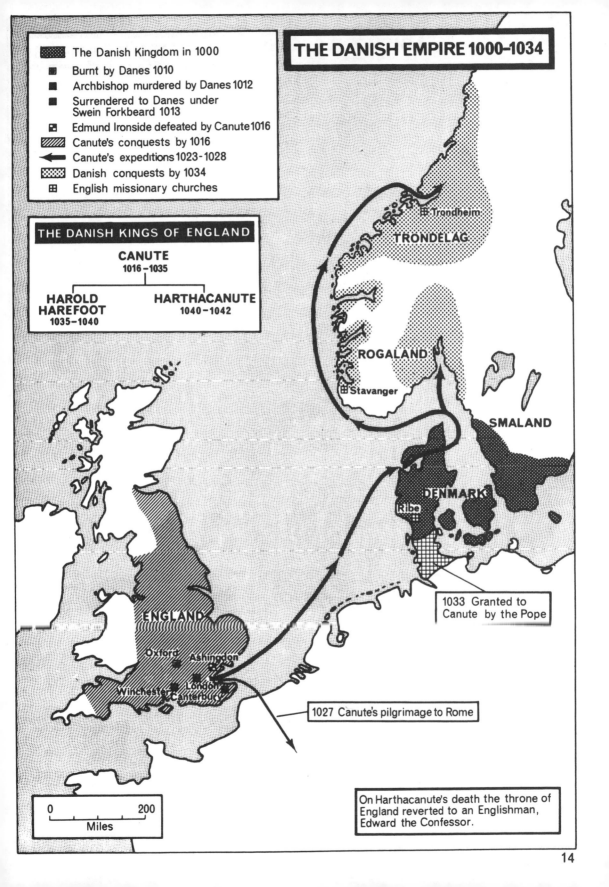

THE DANISH EMPIRE 1000–1034

Legend:

- The Danish Kingdom in 1000
- Burnt by Danes 1010
- Archbishop murdered by Danes 1012
- Surrendered to Danes under Swein Forkbeard 1013
- Edmund Ironside defeated by Canute 1016
- Canute's conquests by 1016
- ← Canute's expeditions 1023-1028
- Danish conquests by 1034
- English missionary churches

THE DANISH KINGS OF ENGLAND

CANUTE
1016–1035

HAROLD HAREFOOT
1035–1040

HARTHACANUTE
1040–1042

Trondheim

TRONDELAG

ROGALAND

Stavanger

SMALAND

DENMARK

Ribe

1033 Granted to Canute by the Pope

ENGLAND

Oxford   Ashingdon

Winchester   London
Canterbury

1027 Canute's pilgrimage to Rome

0   200
Miles

On Harthacanute's death the throne of England reverted to an Englishman, Edward the Confessor.

14

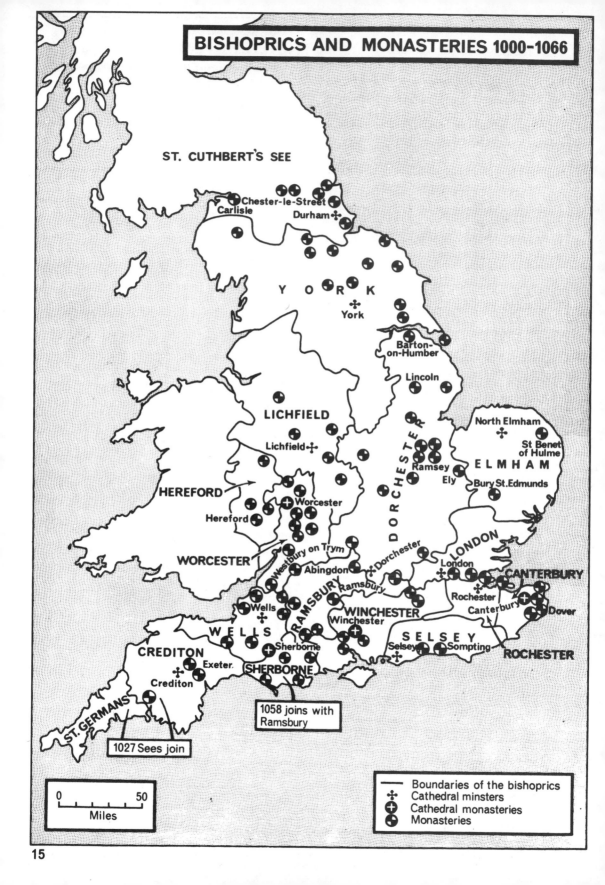

BISHOPRICS AND MONASTERIES 1000-1066

ST. CUTHBERT'S SEE

Carlisle

Chester-le-Street

Durham ✠

Y O R K

York ✠

Barton-on-Humber

Lincoln

LICHFIELD

Lichfield ✠

HEREFORD

Hereford

Worcester ✠

WORCESTER

Westbury on Trym

Abingdon

D O R C H E S T E R

Dorchester ✠

North Elmham ✠

St Benet of Hulme

E L M H A M

Ramsey

Ely

Bury St.Edmunds

LONDON

London ✠

CANTERBURY

Rochester ✠

Canterbury ✠

Dover

RAMSBURY

Ramsbury ✠

Wells

WELLS

WINCHESTER

Winchester ✠

S E L S E Y

Selsey ✠

Sompting

ROCHESTER

CREDITON

Exeter

Crediton ✠

Sherborne ✠

SHERBORNE

ST. GERMANS

1027 Sees join

1058 joins with Ramsbury

0 ——— 50
Miles

Boundaries of the bishoprics
✠ Cathedral minsters
✠ Cathedral monasteries
● Monasteries

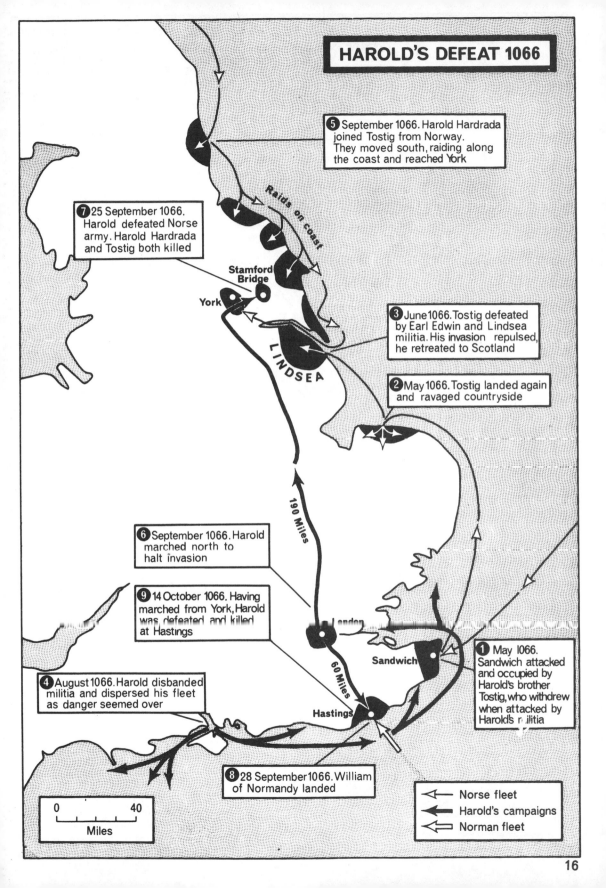

HAROLD'S DEFEAT 1066

5 September 1066. Harold Hardrada joined Tostig from Norway. They moved south, raiding along the coast and reached York

7 25 September 1066. Harold defeated Norse army. Harold Hardrada and Tostig both killed

Raids on coast

Stamford Bridge

York

LINDSEA

3 June 1066. Tostig defeated by Earl Edwin and Lindsea militia. His invasion repulsed, he retreated to Scotland

2 May 1066. Tostig landed again and ravaged countryside

190 Miles

6 September 1066. Harold marched north to halt invasion

9 14 October 1066. Having marched from York, Harold was defeated and killed at Hastings

London

Sandwich

1 May 1066. Sandwich attacked and occupied by Harold's brother Tostig, who withdrew when attacked by Harold's militia

60 Miles

4 August 1066. Harold disbanded militia and dispersed his fleet as danger seemed over

Hastings

8 28 September 1066. William of Normandy landed

◁— Norse fleet
◀— Harold's campaigns
◁— Norman fleet

0   40
Miles

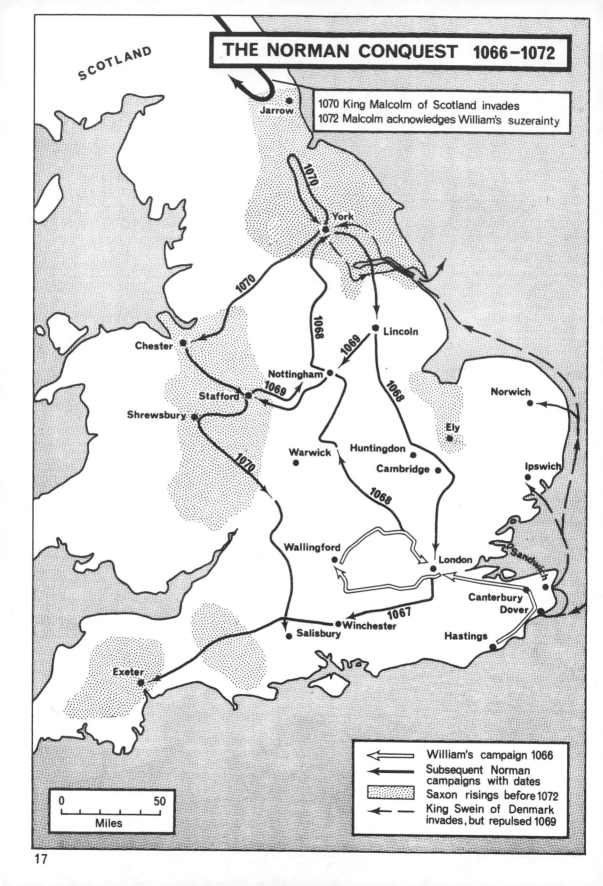

THE NORMAN CONQUEST 1066–1072

SCOTLAND

1070 King Malcolm of Scotland invades
1072 Malcolm acknowledges William's suzerainty

Jarrow

1070

York

1070

Chester

1068

Lincoln

1069

Nottingham

1069

Stafford

Shrewsbury

1068

Norwich

Ely

Ipswich

1070

Warwick

Huntingdon

Cambridge

1068

Wallingford

London

Canterbury
Dover

1068

1067

Winchester

Salisbury

Hastings

Exeter

0   50
Miles

→ William's campaign 1066
→ Subsequent Norman campaigns with dates
▨ Saxon risings before 1072
→– King Swein of Denmark invades, but repulsed 1069

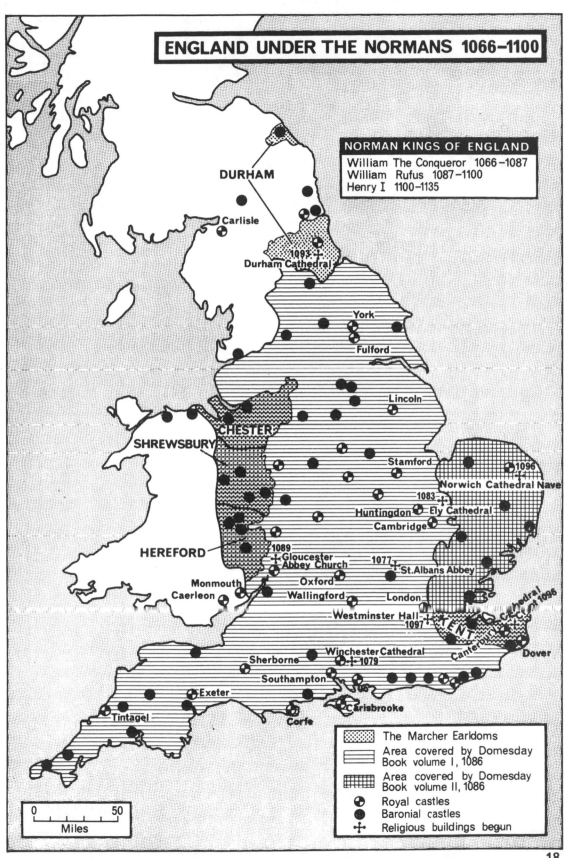

ENGLAND UNDER THE NORMANS 1066–1100

DURHAM

Carlisle

1093 Durham Cathedral

York

Fulford

Lincoln

CHESTER

SHREWSBURY

Stamford

1096
Norwich Cathedral Nave

1083
Huntingdon   Ely Cathedral

Cambridge

HEREFORD

1089
Gloucester
Abbey Church

1077
St. Albans Abbey

Monmouth
Caerleon

Oxford

Wallingford

London

Westminster Hall
1097

KENT

Canterbury Cathedral 1096

Dover

Winchester Cathedral

Sherborne
1079

Southampton

Exeter

Carisbrooke

Tintagel

Corfe

▨	The Marcher Earldoms
▤	Area covered by Domesday Book volume I, 1086
▦	Area covered by Domesday Book volume II, 1086
◍	Royal castles
●	Baronial castles
✛	Religious buildings begun

0   50
Miles

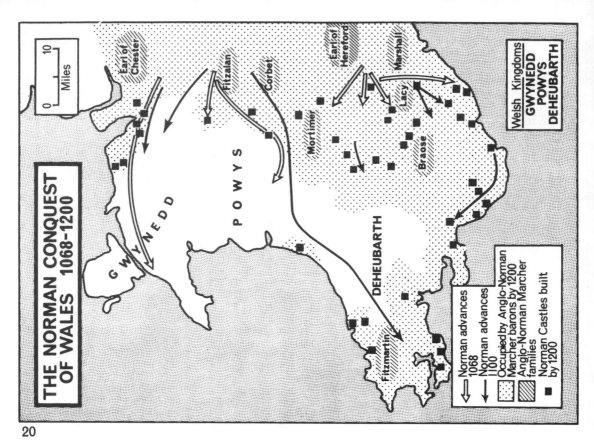

THE NORMAN CONQUEST OF WALES 1068-1200

Welsh Kingdoms
GWYNEDD
POWYS
DEHEUBARTH

Earl of Chester

Fitzalan

Corbet

Earl of Hereford

Marshall

Lacy

Mortimer

Brause

GWYNEDD

POWYS

DEHEUBARTH

Fitzmartin

Miles
0   10

→ Norman advances 1068

→ Norman advances 1100

Occupied by Anglo-Norman Marcher barons by 1200

Anglo-Norman Marcher families

■ Norman Castles built by 1200

20

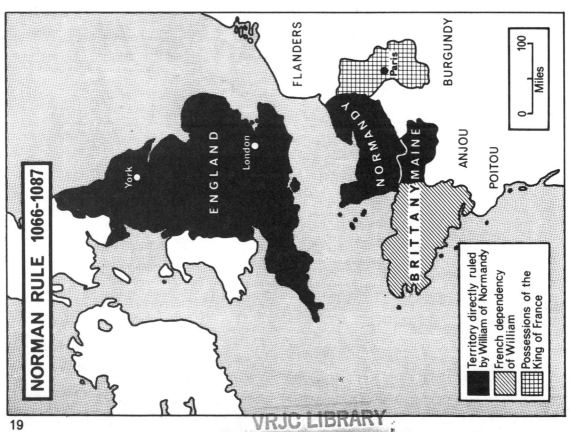

NORMAN RULE 1066-1087

FLANDERS

Paris

BURGUNDY

York

London

ENGLAND

NORMANDY

MAINE

ANJOU

POITOU

BRITTANY

Miles
0   100

Territory directly ruled by William of Normandy

French dependency of William

Possessions of the King of France

19

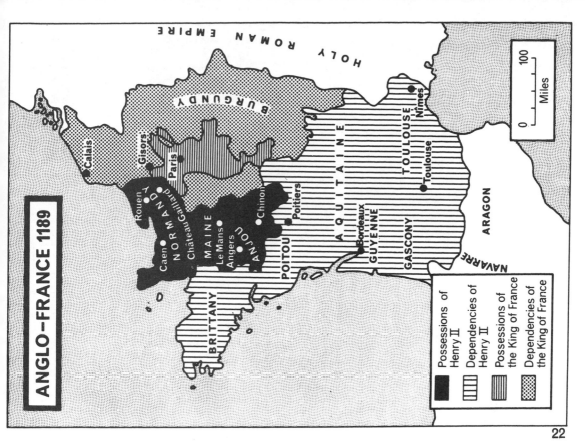

ANGLO–FRANCE 1189

HOLY ROMAN EMPIRE

BURGUNDY

Calais
Gisors
Paris
Rouen
NORMANDY
Château Gaillard
Caen
MAINE
Le Mans
Angers
ANJOU
Chinon
Poitiers
BRITTANY
POITOU
AQUITAINE
Bordeaux
GUYENNE
GASCONY
TOULOUSE
Toulouse
Nîmes
ARAGON
NAVARRE

Possessions of Henry II

Dependencies of Henry II

Possessions of the King of France

Dependencies of the King of France

0 — 100
Miles

22

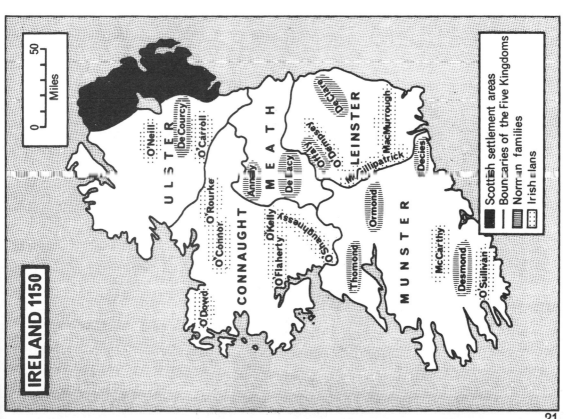

IRELAND 1150

0 — 50
Miles

ULSTER
O'Neill
De Courcy
O'Carroll
O'Rourke
O'Connor
O'Dowd
CONNAUGHT
O'Flaherty
O'Kelly
MEATH
Annaly
De Lacy
O'Shaughnessy
Ossory
Thomond
MUNSTER
McCarthy
Desmond
O'Sullivan
Ormond
O'Dempsey
O'Carroll
O'Toole
O'Byrne
LEINSTER
MacMurrough
MacGillipatrick
Decies

Scottish settlement areas

Boundaries of the Five Kingdoms

Norman families

Irish clans

21

THE CHURCH 1100-1300

The Cistercians stressed manual labour and fieldwork. They introduced many farming improvements and were large exporters of wool. By 1200 there were over 100 Cistercian houses in England.

Furness

Rievaulx

Byland

Ripon Cathedral 1154

York Minster Nave 1291

Fountains

Lincoln Cathedral 1185

Lichfield Cathedral 1280

Tintern

Canterbury Cathedral Choir 1174

Wells Cathedral Nave 1214

Salisbury Cathedral 1220

✚	Cistercian foundations 1127–1180
⊕	Cistercian foundations 1180–1300
✛	Houses of the Dominican friars 1221–1300
⬤	Houses of the Franciscan friars 1230–1300
✤	Other religious buildings begun

0   50
Miles

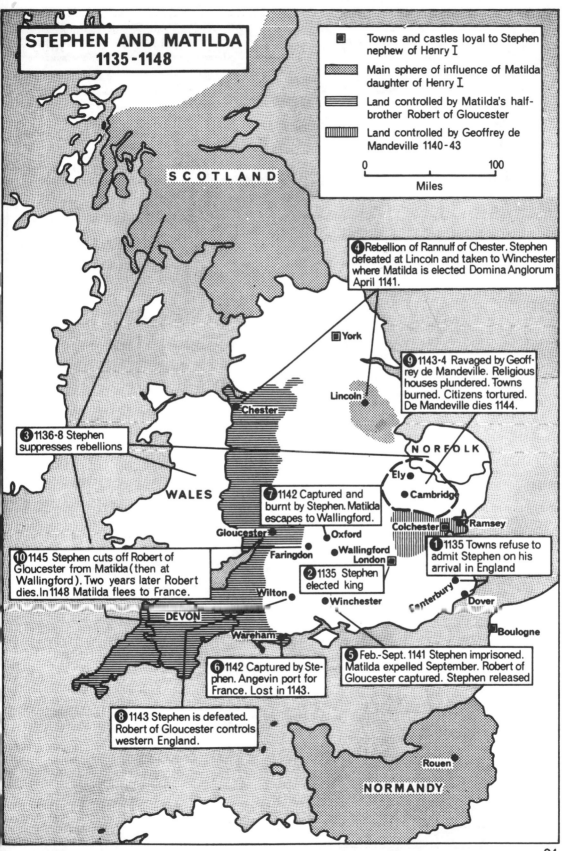

STEPHEN AND MATILDA
1135-1148

Legend:
- Towns and castles loyal to Stephen nephew of Henry I
- Main sphere of influence of Matilda daughter of Henry I
- Land controlled by Matilda's half-brother Robert of Gloucester
- Land controlled by Geoffrey de Mandeville 1140-43

0 — 100 Miles

SCOTLAND

4 Rebellion of Rannulf of Chester. Stephen defeated at Lincoln and taken to Winchester where Matilda is elected Domina Anglorum April 1141.

York

9 1143-4 Ravaged by Geoffrey de Mandeville. Religious houses plundered. Towns burned. Citizens tortured. De Mandeville dies 1144.

Chester

Lincoln

3 1136-8 Stephen suppresses rebellions

NORFOLK

Ely

Cambridge

WALES

7 1142 Captured and burnt by Stephen. Matilda escapes to Wallingford.

Colchester · Ramsey

Gloucester

Oxford

Wallingford

1 1135 Towns refuse to admit Stephen on his arrival in England

Faringdon

London

10 1145 Stephen cuts off Robert of Gloucester from Matilda (then at Wallingford). Two years later Robert dies. In 1148 Matilda flees to France.

2 1135 Stephen elected king

Wilton

Winchester

Canterbury

Dover

DEVON

5 Feb.-Sept. 1141 Stephen imprisoned. Matilda expelled September. Robert of Gloucester captured. Stephen released

Wareham

Boulogne

6 1142 Captured by Stephen. Angevin port for France. Lost in 1143.

8 1143 Stephen is defeated. Robert of Gloucester controls western England.

Rouen

NORMANDY

24

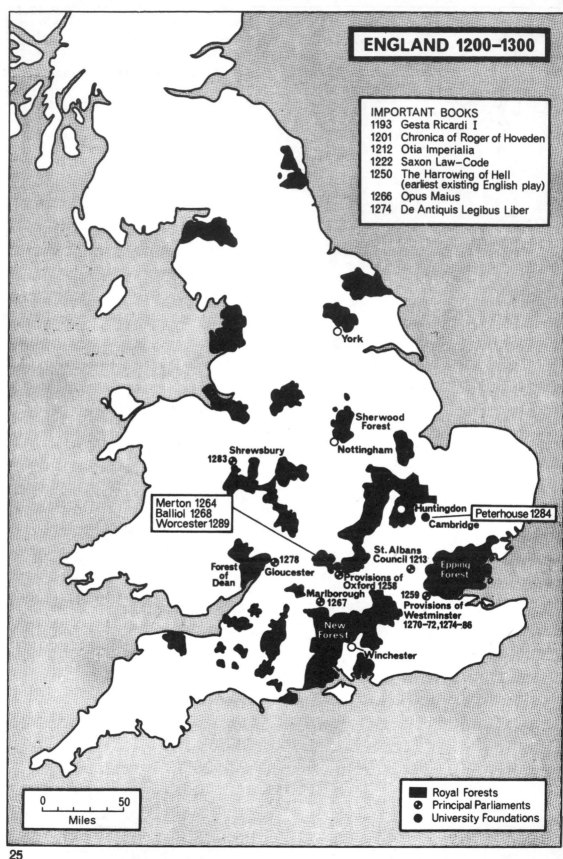

ENGLAND 1200–1300

IMPORTANT BOOKS
1193 Gesta Ricardi I
1201 Chronica of Roger of Hoveden
1212 Otia Imperialia
1222 Saxon Law–Code
1250 The Harrowing of Hell
(earliest existing English play)
1266 Opus Maius
1274 De Antiquis Legibus Liber

York

Sherwood
Forest

Shrewsbury
1283

Nottingham

Merton 1264
Balliol 1268
Worcester 1289

Huntingdon
Peterhouse 1284
Cambridge

St. Albans
Council 1213

1278
Forest
of
Dean

Gloucester

Provisions of
Oxford 1258

Epping
Forest

Marlborough
1267

1259
Provisions of
Westminster
1270–72, 1274–86

New
Forest

Winchester

0   50
Miles

■ Royal Forests
⊕ Principal Parliaments
● University Foundations

25

THE ECONOMY 1200–1300

1245 Papal money-raiser expelled from England by king, clergy and barons
1274 Anglo-Flanders Commercial Treaty
1275 King to receive duty on wool
1280 German merchants in England form a Hansa
1290 Expulsion of the Jews from England
1299 Act to repress bad coinage passed

York
blues
Beverley

Lincoln scarlets
Lincoln

Nottingham
Stamfords
Norwich

Leicester
Stamford
Somersham
Coventry
Huntingdon
Ramsey
Northampton
Bury St.Edmunds
Worcester
Warwick
Cambridge
Ipswich
Bedford
Sudbury
Gloucester
russets
Colchester
russets
Chepstow
Oxford
russets
Wallingford
London
Bristol
Marlborough
Canterbury
Devizes
Hythe
Dover
russets
Romney
Wilton
Winchester
Rye
Salisbury
Winchelsea
Hastings

Cloth producing areas with names of cloth
Towns with weavers guilds by 1200
The Cinque Ports: special liberties granted 1278
The liberties of Chepstow, Ramsey and Somersham
Towns with Jewish settlements where Jewish loans were recorded 1190–1290

0   50
Miles

26

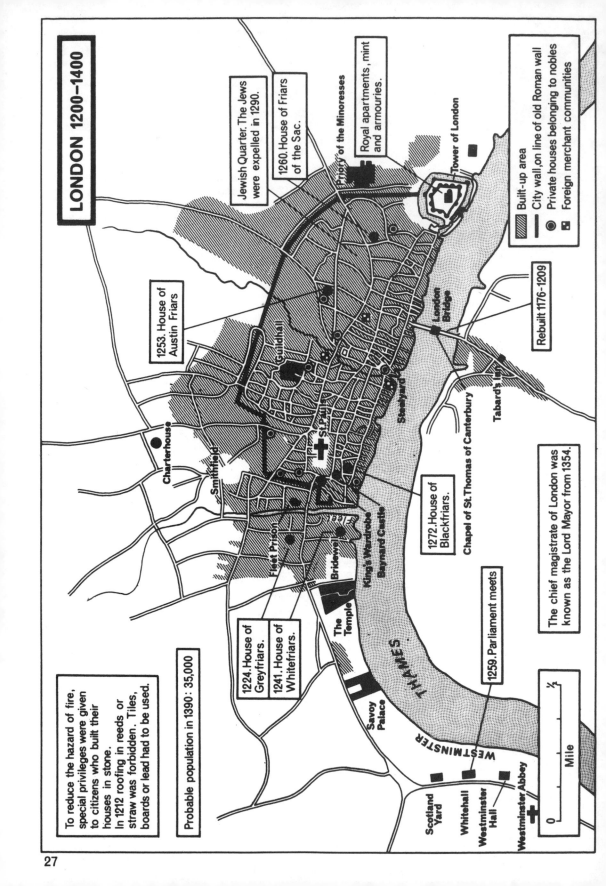

LONDON 1200–1400

Built-up area

— City wall, on line of old Roman wall

● Private houses belonging to nobles

■ Foreign merchant communities

Jewish Quarter. The Jews were expelled in 1290.

1260. House of Friars of the Sac.

Priory of the Minoresses

Royal apartments, mint and armouries.

Tower of London

1253. House of Austin Friars

Guildhall

London Bridge

Rebuilt 1176–1209

Charterhouse

Smithfield

St. Paul's

Steelyard

Tabard's Inn

1272. House of Blackfriars.

Chapel of St. Thomas of Canterbury

The chief magistrate of London was known as the Lord Mayor from 1354.

Fleet Prison

Bridewell

King's Wardrobe
Baynard Castle

1224. House of Greyfriars

1241. House of Whitefriars.

The Temple

1259. Parliament meets

Savoy Palace

THAMES

WESTMINSTER

To reduce the hazard of fire, special privileges were given to citizens who built their houses in stone.
In 1212 roofing in reeds or straw was forbidden. Tiles, boards or lead had to be used.

Probable population in 1390: 35,000

Scotland Yard

Whitehall

Westminster Hall

Westminster Abbey

Mile

0   ½

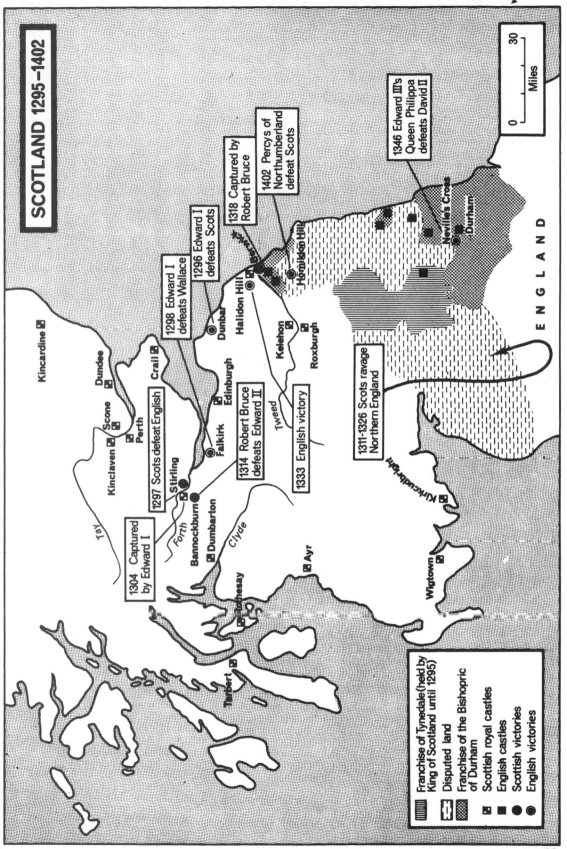

SCOTLAND 1295–1402

0 ___ 30

Miles

1346 Edward III's Queen Philippa defeats David II

1402 Percys of Northumberland defeat Scots

1318 Captured by Robert Bruce

1296 Edward I defeats Scots

1298 Edward I defeats Wallace

Neville's Cross

Durham

Homildon Hill

E N G L A N D

Kincardine

Dundee

Scone

Perth

Crail

Kinclaven

Edinburgh

Dunbar

Halidon Hill

Kelston

Roxburgh

Tay

Falkirk

Stirling

1297 Scots defeat English

1304 Captured by Edward I

Bannockburn

Dumbarton

Forth

Clyde

Tweed

1314 Robert Bruce defeats Edward II

1333 English victory

1311-1326 Scots ravage Northern England

Kirkcudbright

Ayr

Rothesay

Wigtown

Tarbert

Franchise of Tynedale (held by King of Scotland until 1295)

Disputed land

Franchise of the Bishopric of Durham

Scottish royal castles

English castles

Scottish victories

English victories

28

THE HUNDRED YEARS' WAR
1259-1368

0   100
Miles

Calais
Etaples
Crécy
Abbeville

HOLY

Barfleur
Rouen
Caen
NORMANDY
Paris

ROMAN

Bretigny

ANJOU
Tours
Bourges

EMPIRE

Poitiers
POITOU

F
R
A
N
C
E

DAUPHINÉ

AQUITAINE
Bordeaux
GUYENNE

QUERCY
ROUERGUE

GASCONY
Bayonne
Toulouse

Vitoria
Pass of
Roncesvalles
To Burgos
Pamplona
NAVARRE
Narbonne

ARAGON

■ Possessions of Henry III, 1259	⇒⇒ Edward III's campaign 1346-1349
∷ Possessions of the King of France, 1259	the three campaigns of Edward the Black Prince:
▨ English gains 1275	→ to Narbonne 1355
▧ English gains at the Treaty of Bretigny, 1368	--→ to Poitiers 1356
	---→ to Burgos 1367

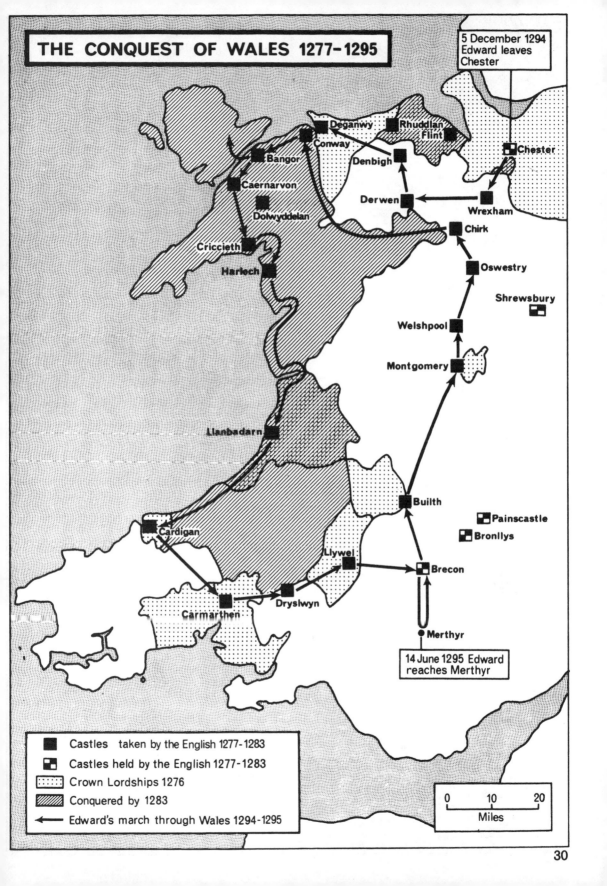

THE CONQUEST OF WALES 1277-1295

5 December 1294
Edward leaves
Chester

Deganwy
Rhuddlan
Flint
Conway
Denbigh
Chester
Bangor
Derwen
Wrexham
Caernarvon
Dolwyddelan
Chirk
Criccieth
Oswestry
Harlech
Shrewsbury
Welshpool
Montgomery
Llanbadarn
Builth
Painscastle
Cardigan
Bronllys
Llywel
Brecon
Dryslwyn
Carmarthen
Merthyr

14 June 1295 Edward
reaches Merthyr

■ Castles taken by the English 1277-1283
◨ Castles held by the English 1277-1283
⋮⋮⋮ Crown Lordships 1276
⫽⫽ Conquered by 1283
← Edward's march through Wales 1294-1295

0   10   20
Miles

30

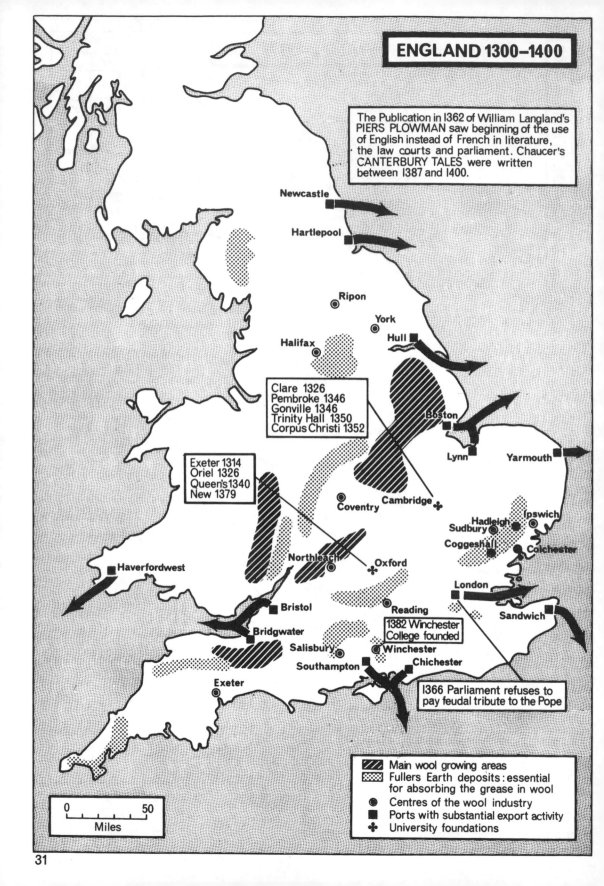

ENGLAND 1300–1400

The Publication in 1362 of William Langland's PIERS PLOWMAN saw beginning of the use of English instead of French in literature, the law courts and parliament. Chaucer's CANTERBURY TALES were written between 1387 and 1400.

Newcastle

Hartlepool

Ripon

York

Hull

Halifax

Clare 1326
Pembroke 1346
Gonville 1346
Trinity Hall 1350
Corpus Christi 1352

Boston

Exeter 1314
Oriel 1326
Queen's 1340
New 1379

Lynn

Yarmouth

Coventry

Cambridge

Hadleigh
Ipswich
Sudbury
Coggeshall
Colchester

Haverfordwest

Northleach

Oxford

London

Bristol

Reading

Sandwich

Bridgwater

1382 Winchester
College founded

Salisbury

Winchester

Chichester

Southampton

Exeter

1366 Parliament refuses to pay feudal tribute to the Pope

Main wool growing areas
Fullers Earth deposits: essential for absorbing the grease in wool
Centres of the wool industry
Ports with substantial export activity
University foundations

0   50
Miles

31

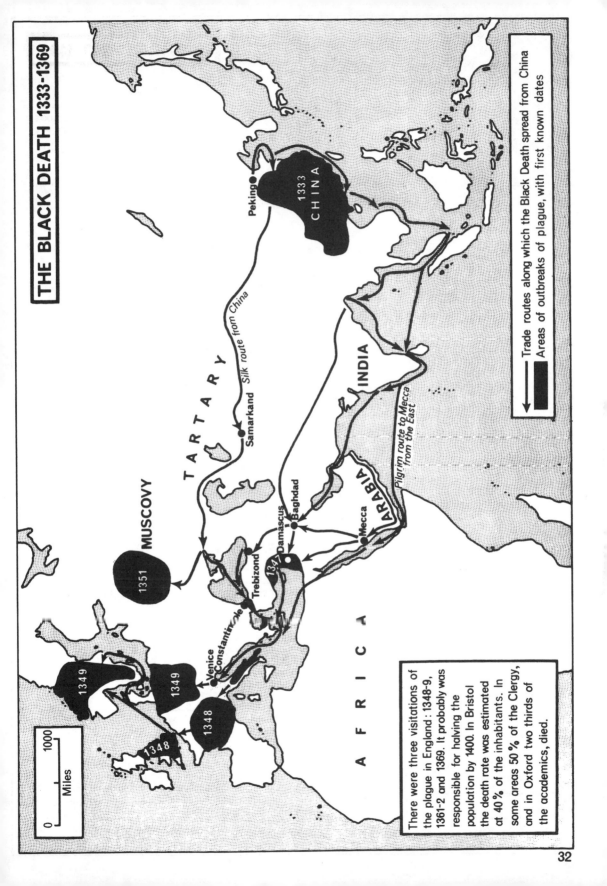

THE BLACK DEATH 1333-1369

CHINA 1333

Peking

Silk route from China

T A R T A R Y

Samarkand

MUSCOVY

1351

Trebizond

Constantinople

Venice

1349

1349

1348

1348

1348

INDIA

Pilgrim route to Mecca from the East

Baghdad

Damascus

1347

Mecca

ARABIA

A F R I C A

Miles
0   1000

→ Trade routes along which the Black Death spread from China
■ Areas of outbreaks of plague, with first known dates

There were three visitations of the plague in England : 1348-9, 1361-2 and 1369. It probably was responsible for halving the population by 1400. In Bristol the death rate was estimated at 40% of the inhabitants. In some areas 50% of the Clergy, and in Oxford two thirds of the academics, died.

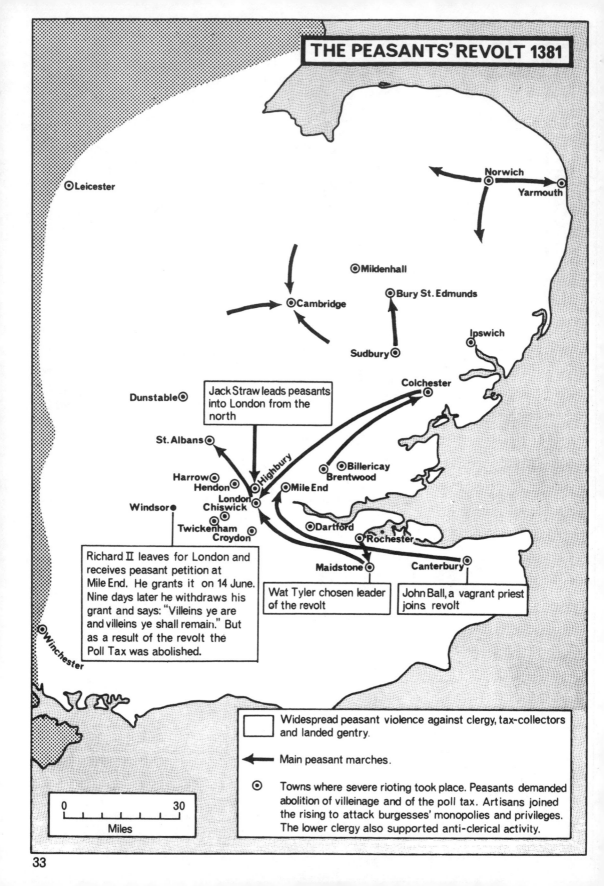

THE PEASANTS' REVOLT 1381

Leicester

Norwich   Yarmouth

Mildenhall

Bury St. Edmunds

Cambridge

Sudbury

Ipswich

Colchester

Dunstable

Jack Straw leads peasants into London from the north

St. Albans

Highbury

Harrow

Hendon

Billericay
Brentwood

London

Mile End

Windsor

Chiswick

Twickenham
Croydon

Dartford

Rochester

Richard II leaves for London and receives peasant petition at Mile End. He grants it on 14 June. Nine days later he withdraws his grant and says: "Villeins ye are and villeins ye shall remain." But as a result of the revolt the Poll Tax was abolished.

Maidstone

Canterbury

Wat Tyler chosen leader of the revolt

John Ball, a vagrant priest joins revolt

Winchester

Widespread peasant violence against clergy, tax-collectors and landed gentry.

← Main peasant marches.

⊙ Towns where severe rioting took place. Peasants demanded abolition of villeinage and of the poll tax. Artisans joined the rising to attack burgesses' monopolies and privileges. The lower clergy also supported anti-clerical activity.

0   30
Miles

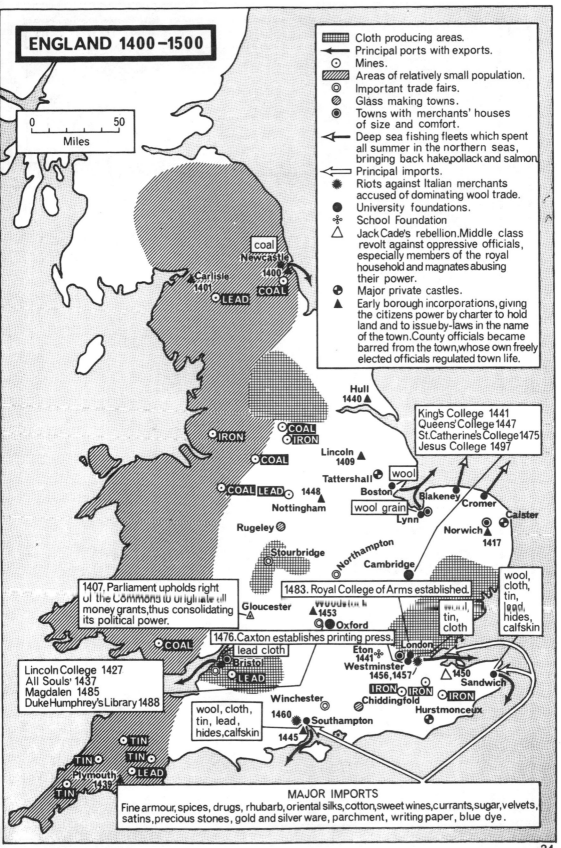

ENGLAND 1400–1500

0 _____ 50
Miles

Cloth producing areas.
Principal ports with exports.
Mines.
Areas of relatively small population.
Important trade fairs.
Glass making towns.
Towns with merchants' houses of size and comfort.
Deep sea fishing fleets which spent all summer in the northern seas, bringing back hake, pollack and salmon
Principal imports.
Riots against Italian merchants accused of dominating wool trade.
University foundations.
School Foundation
Jack Cade's rebellion. Middle class revolt against oppressive officials, especially members of the royal household and magnates abusing their power.
Major private castles.
Early borough incorporations, giving the citizens power by charter to hold land and to issue by-laws in the name of the town. County officials became barred from the town, whose own freely elected officials regulated town life.

coal
Newcastle 1400
COAL
Carlisle 1401
LEAD

Hull 1440

King's College 1441
Queens' College 1447
St. Catherine's College 1475
Jesus College 1497

IRON
COAL
IRON
COAL
Lincoln 1409
Tattershall
wool
Boston
Blakeney
Cromer
Calster
COAL LEAD 1448
Nottingham
wool grain
Lynn
Norwich 1417
Rugeley
Stourbridge
Northampton
Cambridge

1407. Parliament upholds right of the Commons to originate all money grants, thus consolidating its political power.

Gloucester
Woodstock 1453
Oxford

1483. Royal College of Arms established.

wool, cloth, tin, lead, hides, calfskin

wool, tin, cloth

1476. Caxton establishes printing press.

lead cloth
Bristol
LEAD

Lincoln College 1427
All Souls' 1437
Magdalen 1485
Duke Humphrey's Library 1488

Eton 1441
Westminster 1456, 1457
London
1450
Sandwich

IRON IRON IRON
Chiddingfold
Hurstmonceux

Winchester
1460

wool, cloth, tin, lead, hides, calfskin

Southampton
1445

TIN
TIN
LEAD
Plymouth 1439
TIN

MAJOR IMPORTS
Fine armour, spices, drugs, rhubarb, oriental silks, cotton, sweet wines, currants, sugar, velvets, satins, precious stones, gold and silver ware, parchment, writing paper, blue dye.

THE DEFEAT OF OWEN GLENDOWER 1405-1412

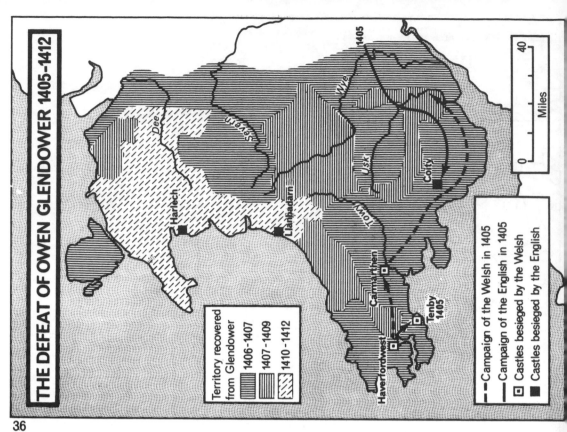

Territory recovered from Glendower
- 1406-1407
- 1407-1409
- 1410-1412

- - - - Campaign of the Welsh in 1405
———— Campaign of the English in 1405
☐ Castles besieged by the Welsh
■ Castles besieged by the English

Miles 0 — 40

Harlech · Llanbadarn · Coity · Carmarthen · Tenby 1405 · Haverfordwest · 1405

Dee · Severn · Wye · Usk · Towy

OWEN GLENDOWER'S REVOLT 1400 – 1405

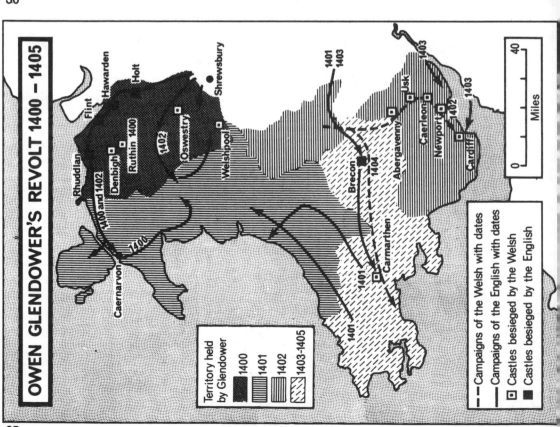

Territory held by Glendower
- 1400
- 1401
- 1402
- 1403-1405

- - - - Campaigns of the Welsh with dates
———— Campaigns of the English with dates
☐ Castles besieged by the Welsh
■ Castles besieged by the English

Miles 0 — 40

Flint · Hawarden · Holt · Shrewsbury · Rhuddlan · Caernarvon · Denbigh · Ruthin 1400 · Oswestry · Welshpool · 1402 · 1400 and 1402 · 1400

Brecon · Abergavenny · Usk · Caerleon · Newport · Cardiff · Carmarthen · 1401 · 1403 · 1404 · 1402

1401 1403

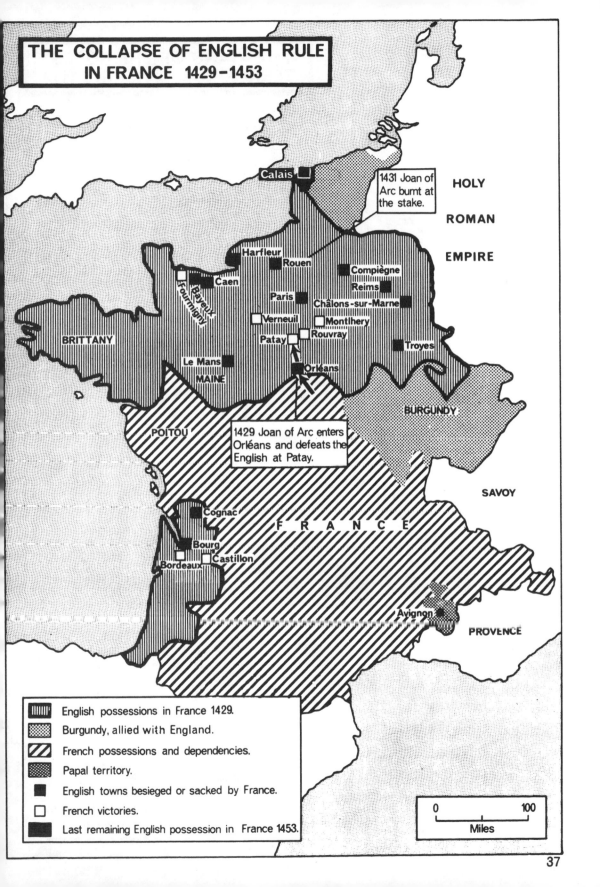

THE COLLAPSE OF ENGLISH RULE IN FRANCE 1429-1453

HOLY

ROMAN

EMPIRE

1431 Joan of Arc burnt at the stake.

Calais

Harfleur

Rouen

Compiègne

Caen

Bayeux

Fourmigny

Reims

Paris

Châlons-sur-Marne

Verneuil

Montlhery

Patay

Rouvray

Troyes

Le Mans

Orléans

MAINE

BRITTANY

BURGUNDY

POITOU

1429 Joan of Arc enters Orléans and defeats the English at Patay.

SAVOY

Cognac

F R A N C E

Bourg

Castillon

Bordeaux

Avignon

PROVENCE

English possessions in France 1429.

Burgundy, allied with England.

French possessions and dependencies.

Papal territory.

English towns besieged or sacked by France.

French victories.

Last remaining English possession in France 1453.

0   100

Miles

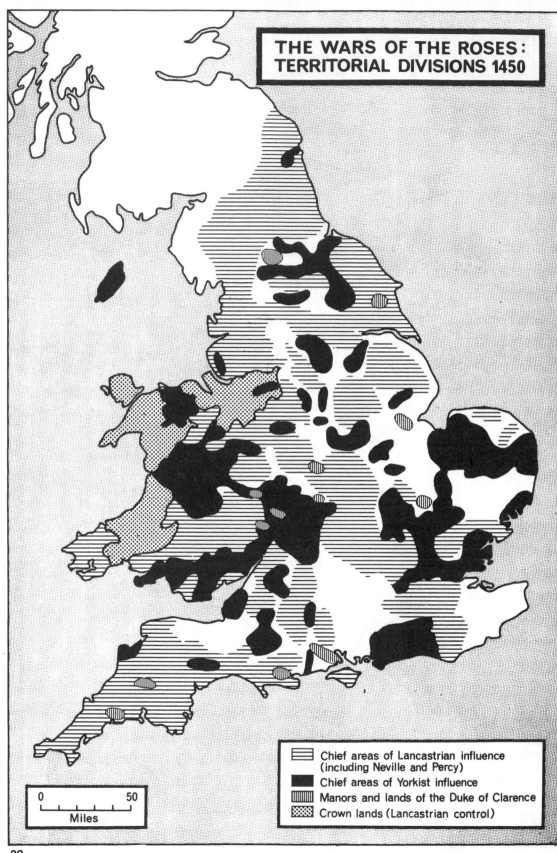

THE WARS OF THE ROSES:
TERRITORIAL DIVISIONS 1450

0   50
Miles

Chief areas of Lancastrian influence
(including Neville and Percy)
Chief areas of Yorkist influence
Manors and lands of the Duke of Clarence
Crown lands (Lancastrian control)

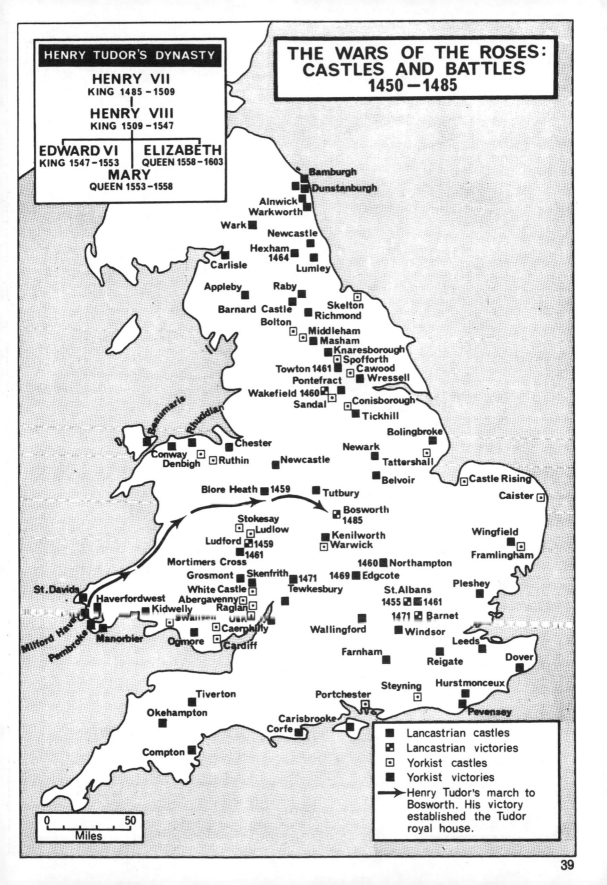

THE WARS OF THE ROSES: CASTLES AND BATTLES 1450—1485

HENRY TUDOR'S DYNASTY

HENRY VII
KING 1485—1509

HENRY VIII
KING 1509—1547

EDWARD VI
KING 1547—1553

ELIZABETH
QUEEN 1558—1603

MARY
QUEEN 1553—1558

Bamburgh
Dunstanburgh
Alnwick
Warkworth
Wark
Newcastle
Hexham 1464
Lumley
Carlisle
Appleby
Raby
Barnard Castle
Skelton
Richmond
Bolton
Middleham
Masham
Knaresborough
Towton 1461
Spofforth
Cawood
Pontefract
Wressell
Wakefield 1460
Sandal
Conisborough
Tickhill
Bolingbroke
Chester
Newark
Conway
Denbigh
Ruthin
Newcastle
Tattershall
Belvoir
Castle Rising
Blore Heath 1459
Tutbury
Caister
Bosworth 1485
Stokesay
Ludlow
Kenilworth
Wingfield
Ludford 1459
Warwick
1461
Northampton
Framlingham
Mortimers Cross
1460
Grosmont
Skenfrith
1469 Edgcote
White Castle
1471
Pleshey
St.Davids
Tewkesbury
St.Albans
Haverfordwest
Abergavenny
Raglan
1455
1461
Kidwelly
Swansea
1471 Barnet
Pembroke
Caerphilly
Windsor
Manorbier
Ogmore
Cardiff
Wallingford
Leeds
Farnham
Dover
Reigate
Tiverton
Steyning
Hurstmonceux
Portchester
Okehampton
Carisbrooke
Pevensey
Corfe
Compton

Beaumaris
Rhuddlan
Milford Haven

■ Lancastrian castles
▨ Lancastrian victories
☐ Yorkist castles
■ Yorkist victories
→ Henry Tudor's march to Bosworth. His victory established the Tudor royal house.

0   50
Miles

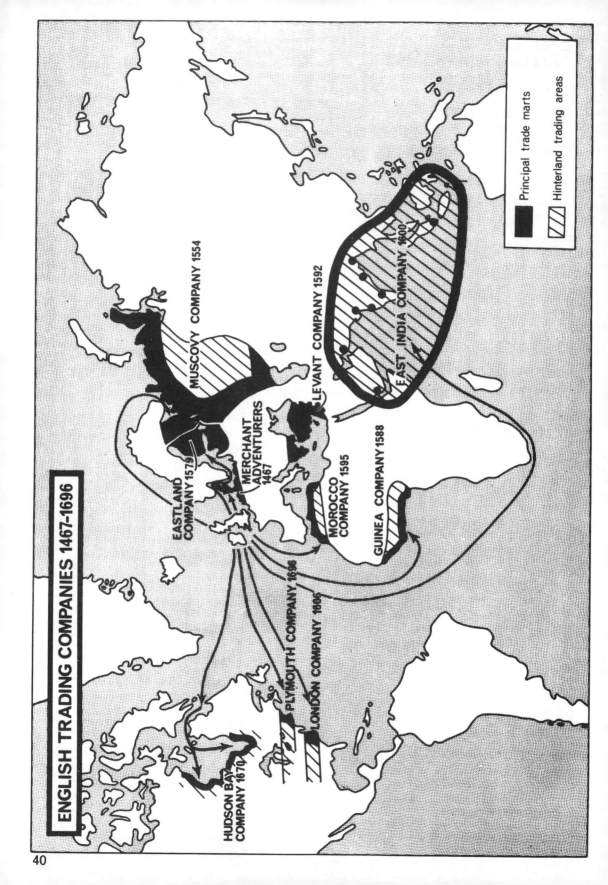

ENGLISH TRADING COMPANIES 1467-1696

MUSCOVY COMPANY 1554

LEVANT COMPANY 1592

EAST INDIA COMPANY 1600

MERCHANT ADVENTURERS 1467

EASTLAND COMPANY 1579

MOROCCO COMPANY 1595

GUINEA COMPANY 1588

PLYMOUTH COMPANY 1606

LONDON COMPANY 1606

HUDSON BAY COMPANY 1670

Principal trade marts

Hinterland trading areas

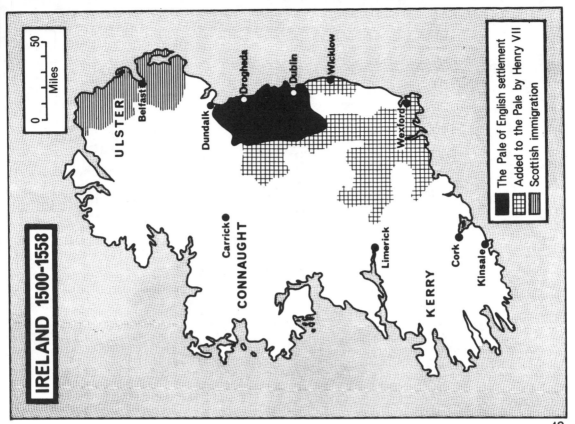

IRELAND 1500-1558

ULSTER

Belfast

Dundalk

Drogheda

Dublin

Wicklow

Wexford

Carrick

CONNAUGHT

Limerick

KERRY

Cork

Kinsale

Miles
0 50

- The Pale of English settlement
- Added to the Pale by Henry VII
- Scottish immigration

42

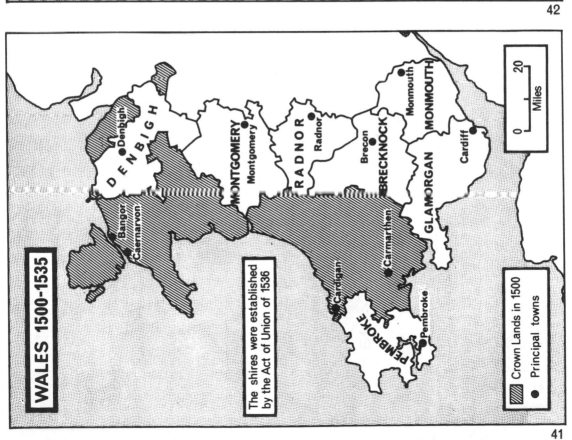

WALES 1500-1535

DENBIGH

Denbigh

Bangor

Caernarvon

MONTGOMERY

Montgomery

RADNOR

Radnor

Brecon

BRECKNOCK

Monmouth

MONMOUTH

GLAMORGAN

Cardiff

Cardigan

Carmarthen

PEMBROKE

Pembroke

The shires were established
by the Act of Union of 1536

Miles
0 20

- Crown Lands in 1500
- Principal towns

41

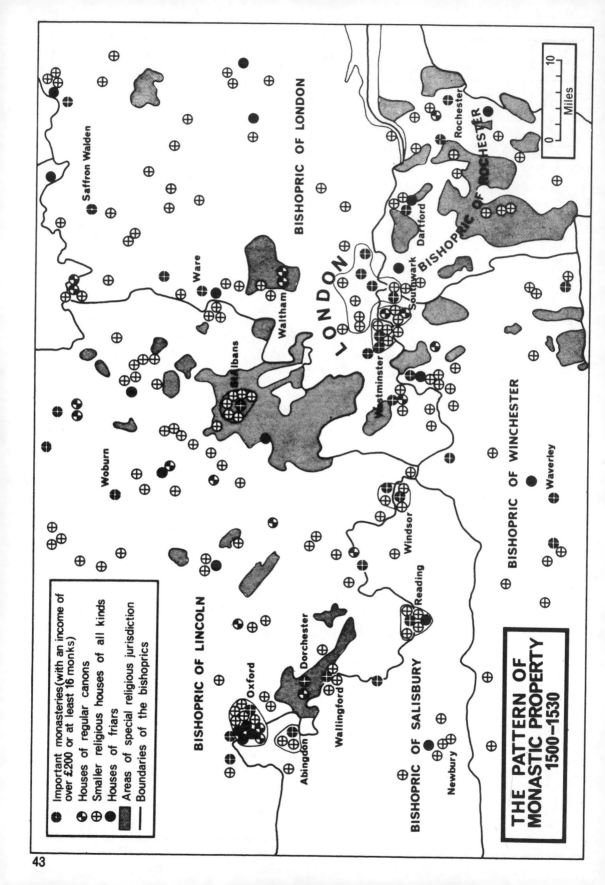

THE PATTERN OF
MONASTIC PROPERTY
1500–1530

Legend:
- Important monasteries (with an income of over £200 or at least 16 monks)
- Houses of regular canons
- Smaller religious houses of all kinds
- Houses of friars
- Areas of special religious jurisdiction
- Boundaries of the bishoprics

BISHOPRIC OF LONDON
BISHOPRIC OF ROCHESTER
BISHOPRIC OF WINCHESTER
BISHOPRIC OF LINCOLN
BISHOPRIC OF SALISBURY

LONDON

Saffron Walden
Ware
Waltham
St Albans
Woburn
Westminster
Southwark
Dartford
Rochester
Windsor
Reading
Dorchester
Oxford
Wallingford
Abingdon
Newbury
Waverley

Miles
0 10

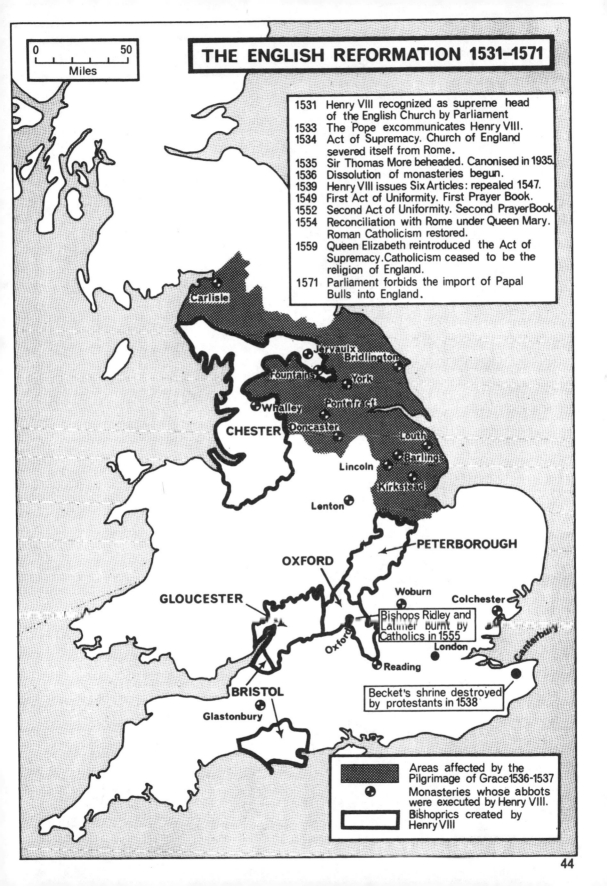

THE ENGLISH REFORMATION 1531–1571

0 — 50 Miles

1531	Henry VIII recognized as supreme head of the English Church by Parliament
1533	The Pope excommunicates Henry VIII.
1534	Act of Supremacy. Church of England severed itself from Rome.
1535	Sir Thomas More beheaded. Canonised in 1935.
1536	Dissolution of monasteries begun.
1539	Henry VIII issues Six Articles: repealed 1547.
1549	First Act of Uniformity. First Prayer Book.
1552	Second Act of Uniformity. Second Prayer Book
1554	Reconciliation with Rome under Queen Mary. Roman Catholicism restored.
1559	Queen Elizabeth reintroduced the Act of Supremacy. Catholicism ceased to be the religion of England.
1571	Parliament forbids the import of Papal Bulls into England.

Carlisle

Jervaulx Bridlington

Fountains York

Whalley Pontefract

CHESTER Doncaster

Louth

Barlings

Lincoln

Kirkstead

Lenton

PETERBOROUGH

OXFORD

GLOUCESTER Woburn Colchester

Bishops Ridley and Latimer burnt by Catholics in 1555

Oxford London

Reading Canterbury

BRISTOL Becket's shrine destroyed by protestants in 1538

Glastonbury

Areas affected by the Pilgrimage of Grace 1536–1537

Monasteries whose abbots were executed by Henry VIII.

Bishoprics created by Henry VIII

44

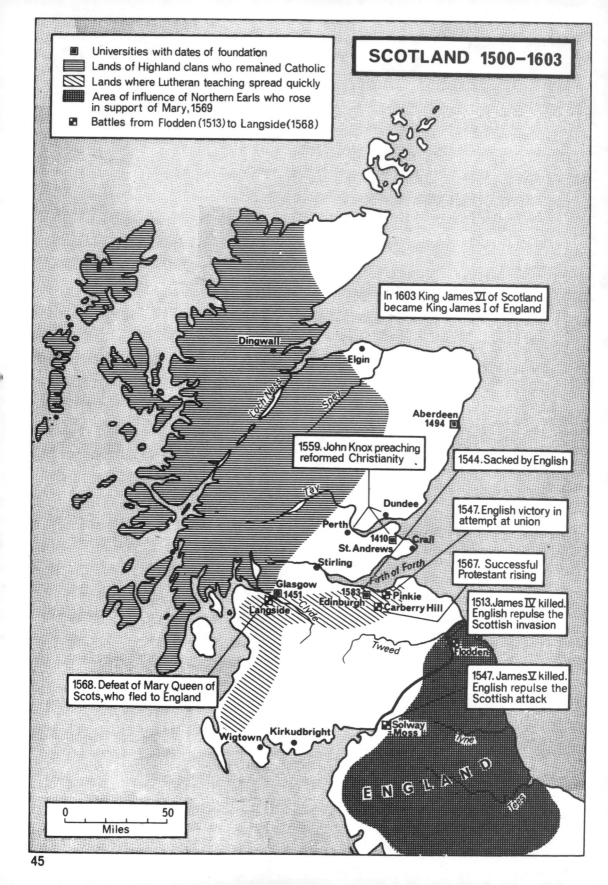

SCOTLAND 1500–1603

Legend:
- Universities with dates of foundation
- Lands of Highland clans who remained Catholic
- Lands where Lutheran teaching spread quickly
- Area of influence of Northern Earls who rose in support of Mary, 1569
- Battles from Flodden (1513) to Langside (1568)

In 1603 King James VI of Scotland became King James I of England

1559. John Knox preaching reformed Christianity

1544. Sacked by English

1547. English victory in attempt at union

1567. Successful Protestant rising

1513. James IV killed. English repulse the Scottish invasion

1547. James V killed. English repulse the Scottish attack

1568. Defeat of Mary Queen of Scots, who fled to England

Dingwall

Elgin

Loch Ness

Spey

Aberdeen 1494

Tay

Dundee

Perth

1410 St. Andrews Crail

Stirling

Glasgow 1451

Langside

Clyde

1583 Edinburgh

Pinkie
Carberry Hill

Firth of Forth

Tweed

Flodden

Solway Moss

Wigtown

Kirkudbright

Tyne

ENGLAND

Tees

0   50
Miles

45

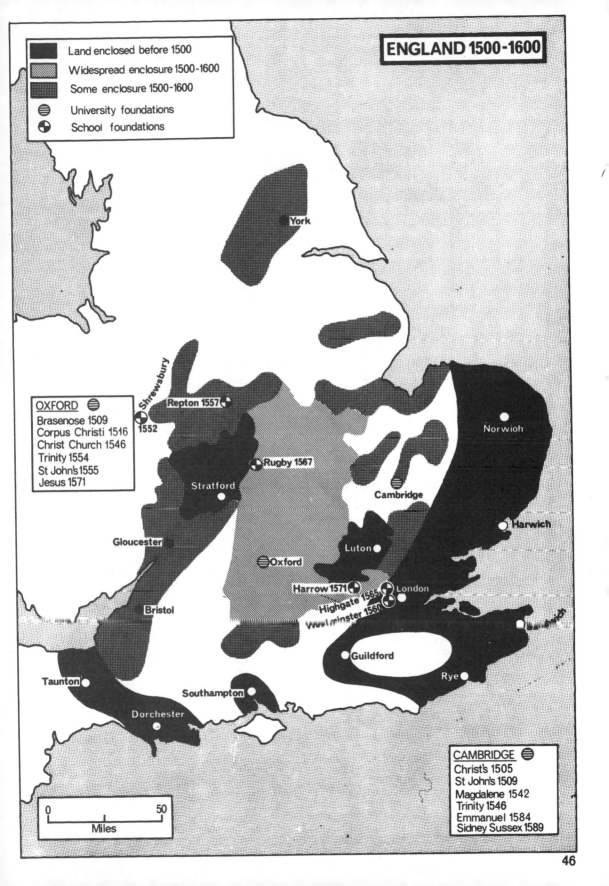

ENGLAND 1500-1600

Land enclosed before 1500
Widespread enclosure 1500-1600
Some enclosure 1500-1600
University foundations
School foundations

OXFORD
Brasenose 1509
Corpus Christi 1516
Christ Church 1546
Trinity 1554
St John's 1555
Jesus 1571

CAMBRIDGE
Christ's 1505
St John's 1509
Magdalene 1542
Trinity 1546
Emmanuel 1584
Sidney Sussex 1589

York

Shrewsbury
Repton 1557
1552
Rugby 1567
Stratford
Norwioh
Cambridge
Gloucester
Luton
Harwich
Oxford
Harrow 1571
Highgate 1565
London
Bristol
Westminster 1560
Guildford
Rye
Taunton
Southampton
Dorchester

0   50
Miles

46

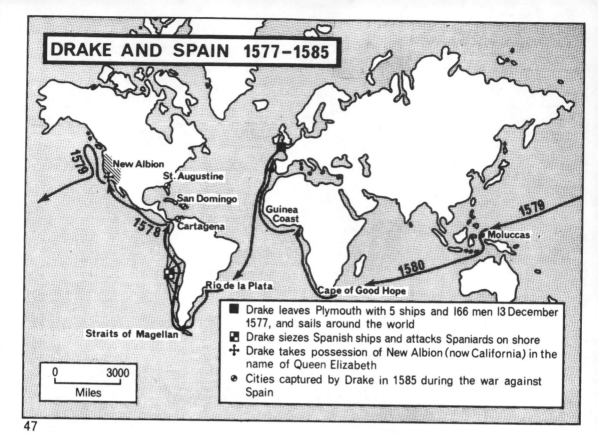

DRAKE AND SPAIN 1577-1585

New Albion
St. Augustine
San Domingo
Cartagena
Guinea Coast
Moluccas
1579
1578
1580
1579
Rio de la Plata
Cape of Good Hope
Straits of Magellan

■ Drake leaves Plymouth with 5 ships and 166 men 13 December 1577, and sails around the world

▣ Drake siezes Spanish ships and attacks Spaniards on shore

✛ Drake takes possession of New Albion (now California) in the name of Queen Elizabeth

● Cities captured by Drake in 1585 during the war against Spain

0 ———— 3000
Miles

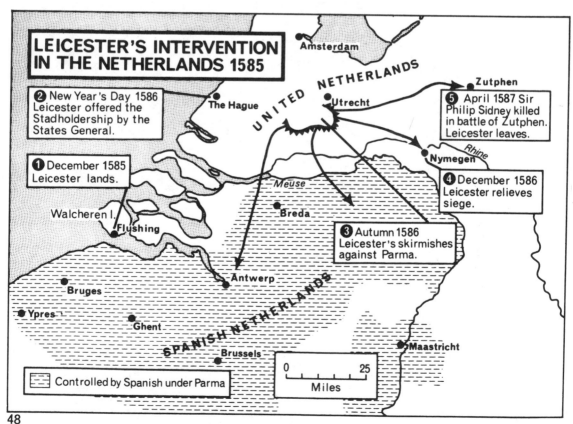

LEICESTER'S INTERVENTION IN THE NETHERLANDS 1585

Amsterdam

UNITED NETHERLANDS

❷ New Year's Day 1586 Leicester offered the Stadholdership by the States General.

The Hague
Utrecht
Zutphen

❺ April 1587 Sir Philip Sidney killed in battle of Zutphen. Leicester leaves.

❶ December 1585 Leicester lands.

Rhine
Nymegen

❹ December 1586 Leicester relieves siege.

Walcheren I.
Flushing

Meuse
Breda

❸ Autumn 1586 Leicester's skirmishes against Parma.

Antwerp

SPANISH NETHERLANDS

Bruges

Ypres
Ghent

Maastricht

Brussels

⬚ Controlled by Spanish under Parma

0 ———— 25
Miles

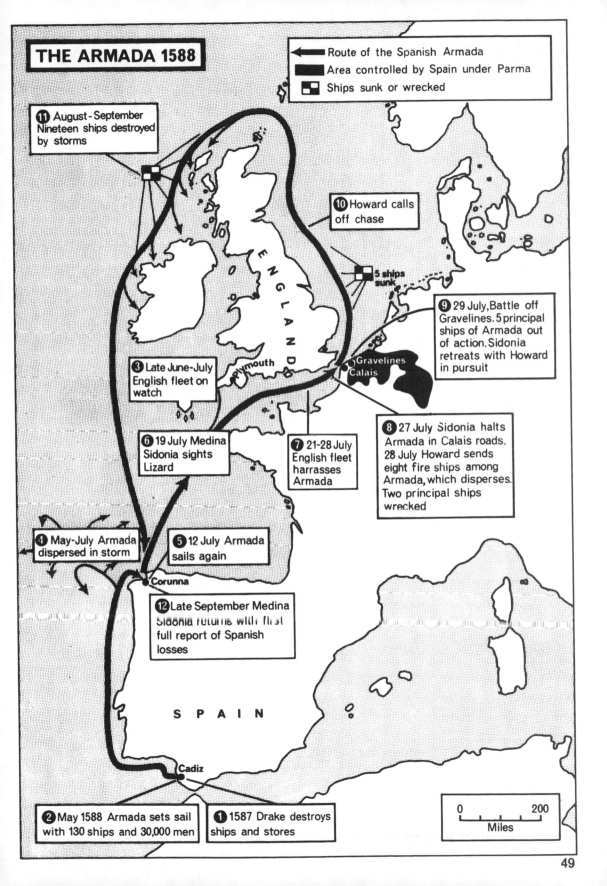

THE ARMADA 1588

Route of the Spanish Armada
Area controlled by Spain under Parma
Ships sunk or wrecked

11 August - September Nineteen ships destroyed by storms

10 Howard calls off chase

5 ships sunk

9 29 July, Battle off Gravelines. 5 principal ships of Armada out of action. Sidonia retreats with Howard in pursuit

3 Late June-July English fleet on watch

ENGLAND

Plymouth

Gravelines
Calais

8 27 July Sidonia halts Armada in Calais roads. 28 July Howard sends eight fire ships among Armada, which disperses. Two principal ships wrecked

6 19 July Medina Sidonia sights Lizard

7 21-28 July English fleet harrasses Armada

1 May-July Armada dispersed in storm

5 12 July Armada sails again

Corunna

12 Late September Medina Sidonia returns with first full report of Spanish losses

S P A I N

Cadiz

2 May 1588 Armada sets sail with 130 ships and 30,000 men

1 1587 Drake destroys ships and stores

0   200
Miles

49

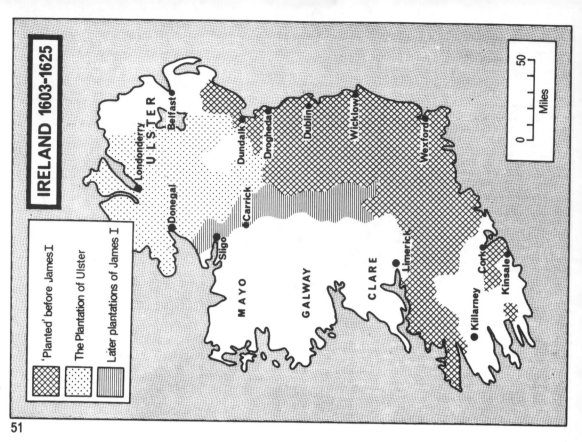

IRELAND 1603-1625

ULSTER

Londonderry
Belfast
Donegal
Sligo
Dundalk
Carrick
Drogheda
Dublin
Wicklow
Wexford
Limerick
Killarney
Cork
Kinsale

MAYO
GALWAY
CLARE

Legend:
- 'Planted' before James I
- The Plantation of Ulster
- Later plantations of James I

0 50 Miles

51

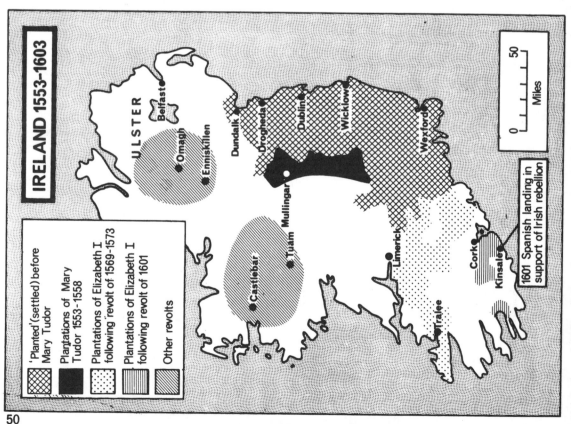

IRELAND 1553-1603

ULSTER

Belfast
Omagh
Enniskillen
Dundalk
Drogheda
Dublin
Wicklow
Wexford
Castlebar
Tuam
Mullingar
Limerick
Tralee
Cork
Kinsale

Legend:
- 'Planted' (settled) before Mary Tudor
- Plantations of Mary Tudor 1553-1558
- Plantations of Elizabeth I following revolt of 1569-1573
- Plantations of Elizabeth I following revolt of 1601
- Other revolts

1601 Spanish landing in support of Irish rebellion

0 50 Miles

50

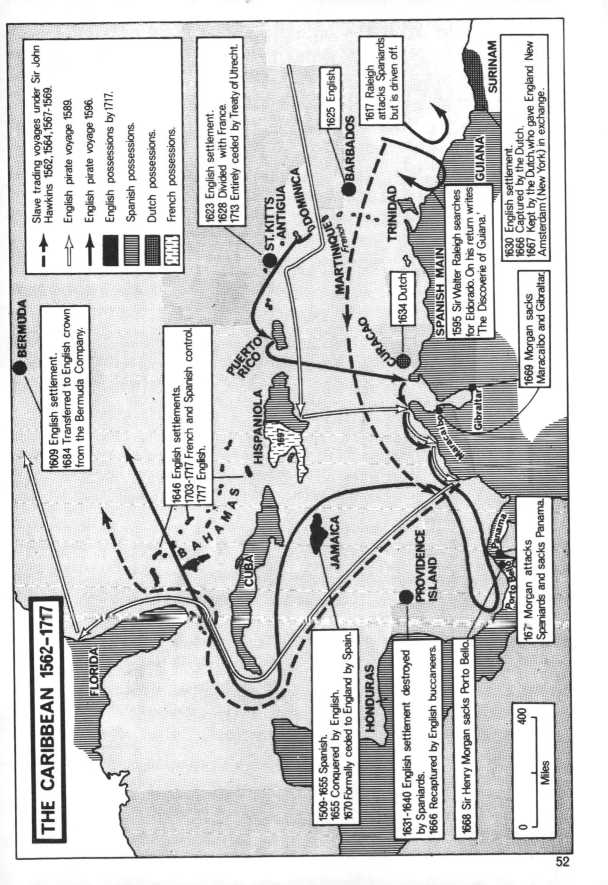

THE CARIBBEAN 1562–1717

Slave trading voyages under Sir John Hawkins 1562,1564,1567-1569.

English pirate voyage 1589.

English pirate voyage 1596.

English possessions by 1717.

Spanish possessions.

Dutch possessions.

French possessions.

BERMUDA
1609 English settlement.
1684 Transferred to English crown from the Bermuda Company.

ST. KITTS
ANTIGUA
1623 English settlement.
1628 Divided with France.
1713 Entirely ceded by Treaty of Utrecht.

DOMINICA

MARTINIQUE French.
1634 Dutch

BARBADOS
1625 English

1617 Raleigh attacks Spaniards but is driven off.

SURINAM

GUIANA
1630 English settlement.
1666 Captured by the Dutch.
1667 Kept by the Dutch, who gave England New Amsterdam (New York) in exchange.

1595 Sir Walter Raleigh searches for Eldorado. On his return writes 'The Discoverie of Guiana.'

TRINIDAD

CURACAO

SPANISH MAIN

PUERTO RICO

HISPANIOLA 1697

BAHAMAS
1646 English settlements.
1703-1717 French and Spanish control.
1717 English.

CUBA

JAMAICA
1509-1655 Spanish.
1655 Conquered by English.
1670 Formally ceded to England by Spain.

FLORIDA

HONDURAS

PROVIDENCE ISLAND
1631-1640 English settlement destroyed by Spaniards.
1666 Recaptured by English buccaneers.

Gibraltar

1669 Morgan sacks Maracaibo and Gibraltar.

Maracaibo

Porto Bello
Panama

1671 Morgan attacks Spaniards and sacks Panama.

1668 Sir Henry Morgan sacks Porto Bello.

0   400
Miles

52

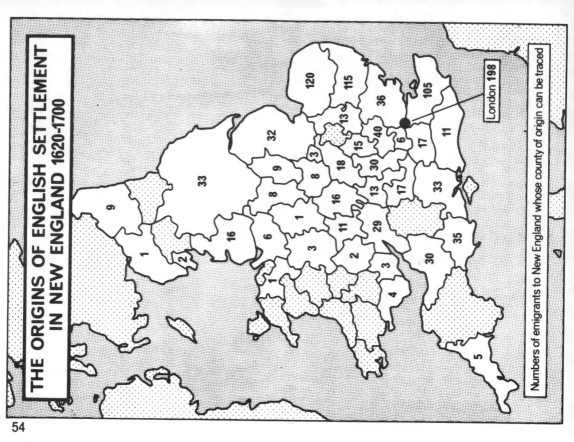

THE ORIGINS OF ENGLISH SETTLEMENT IN NEW ENGLAND 1620-1700

London 198

Numbers of emigrants to New England whose county of origin can be traced

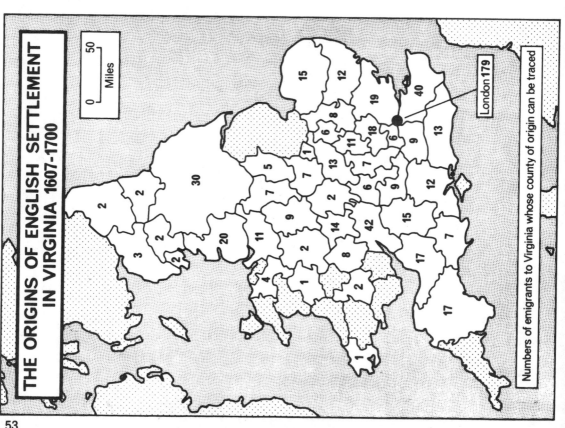

THE ORIGINS OF ENGLISH SETTLEMENT IN VIRGINIA 1607-1700

0   50
Miles

London 179

Numbers of emigrants to Virginia whose county of origin can be traced

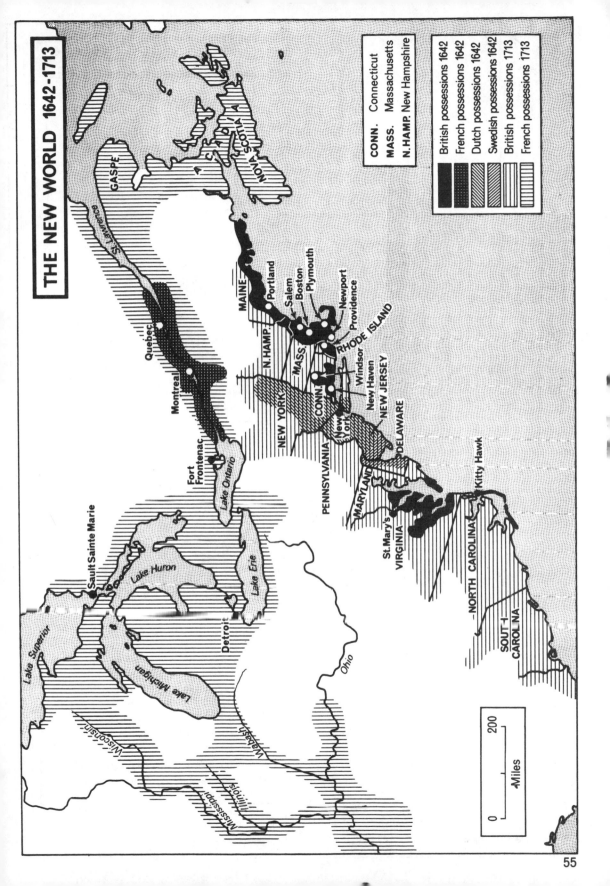

THE NEW WORLD 1642-1713

CONN. Connecticut
MASS. Massachusetts
N.HAMP. New Hampshire

British possessions 1642
French possessions 1642
Dutch possessions 1642
Swedish possessions 1642
British possessions 1713
French possessions 1713

GASPE

CANADA

NOVA SCOTIA

St. Lawrence

Quebec

Montreal

Fort Frontenac

Lake Ontario

Lake Erie

Sault Sainte Marie

Lake Superior

Lake Huron

Lake Michigan

Detroit

Wisconsin

Mississippi

Illinois

Wabash

Ohio

MAINE

N.HAMP.

MASS.

Portland
Salem
Boston
Plymouth
Newport
Providence
RHODE ISLAND

Windsor
New Haven

NEW YORK

CONN.

New York

NEW JERSEY

DELAWARE

PENNSYLVANIA

MARYLAND

St. Mary's

VIRGINIA

Kitty Hawk

NORTH CAROLINA

SOUTH CAROLINA

0   200
Miles

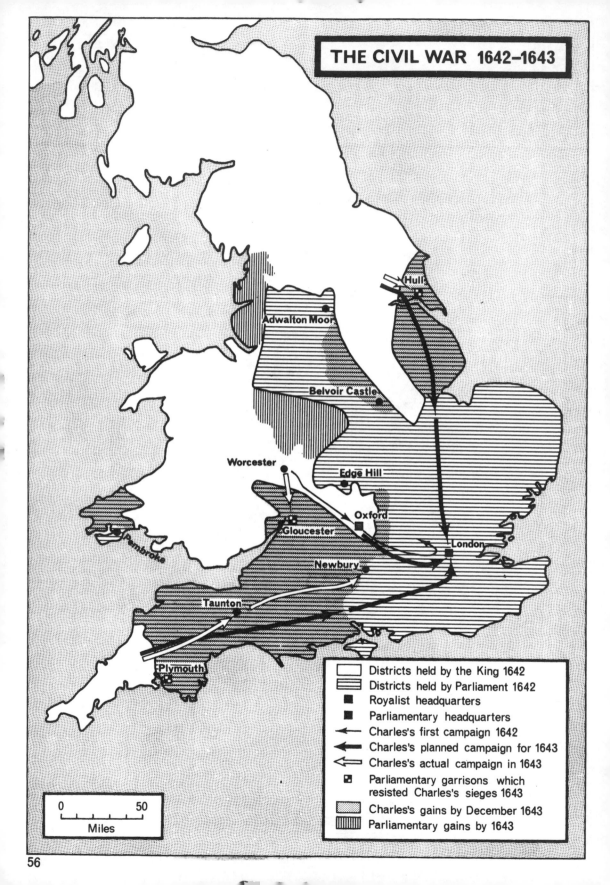

THE CIVIL WAR 1642–1643

Hull

Adwalton Moor

Belvoir Castle

Worcester

Edge Hill

Oxford

Gloucester

Pembroke

London

Newbury

Taunton

Plymouth

	Districts held by the King 1642
	Districts held by Parliament 1642
■	Royalist headquarters
■	Parliamentary headquarters
←	Charles's first campaign 1642
←	Charles's planned campaign for 1643
⇐	Charles's actual campaign in 1643
⊠	Parliamentary garrisons which resisted Charles's sieges 1643
	Charles's gains by December 1643
	Parliamentary gains by 1643

0   50
Miles

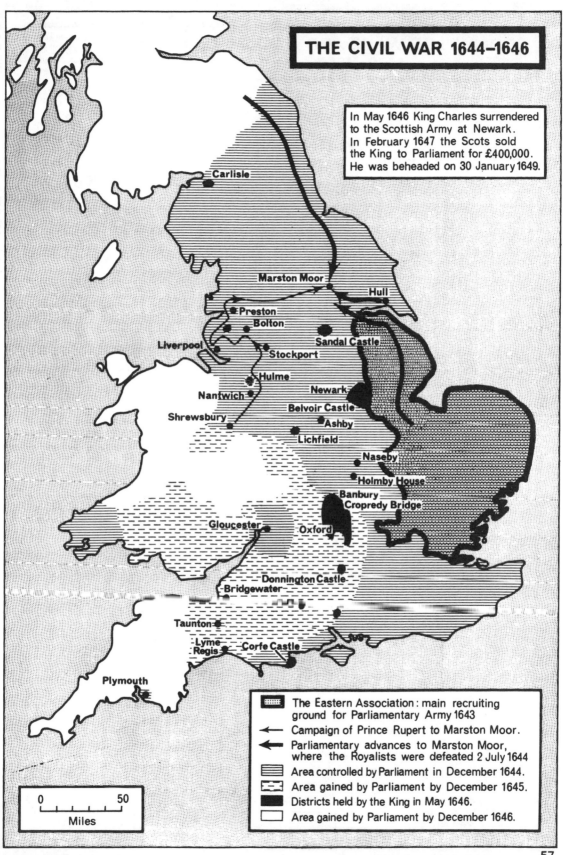

THE CIVIL WAR 1644–1646

In May 1646 King Charles surrendered to the Scottish Army at Newark. In February 1647 the Scots sold the King to Parliament for £400,000. He was beheaded on 30 January 1649.

Carlisle

Marston Moor

Hull

Preston
Bolton

Liverpool
Stockport
Sandal Castle

Hulme

Nantwich
Newark
Shrewsbury
Belvoir Castle
Ashby
Lichfield

Naseby

Holmby House
Banbury
Cropredy Bridge

Gloucester
Oxford

Donnington Castle
Bridgewater

Taunton
Lyme Regis
Corfe Castle

Plymouth

The Eastern Association: main recruiting ground for Parliamentary Army 1643
Campaign of Prince Rupert to Marston Moor.
Parliamentary advances to Marston Moor, where the Royalists were defeated 2 July 1644
Area controlled by Parliament in December 1644.
Area gained by Parliament by December 1645.
Districts held by the King in May 1646.
Area gained by Parliament by December 1646.

0   50
Miles

57

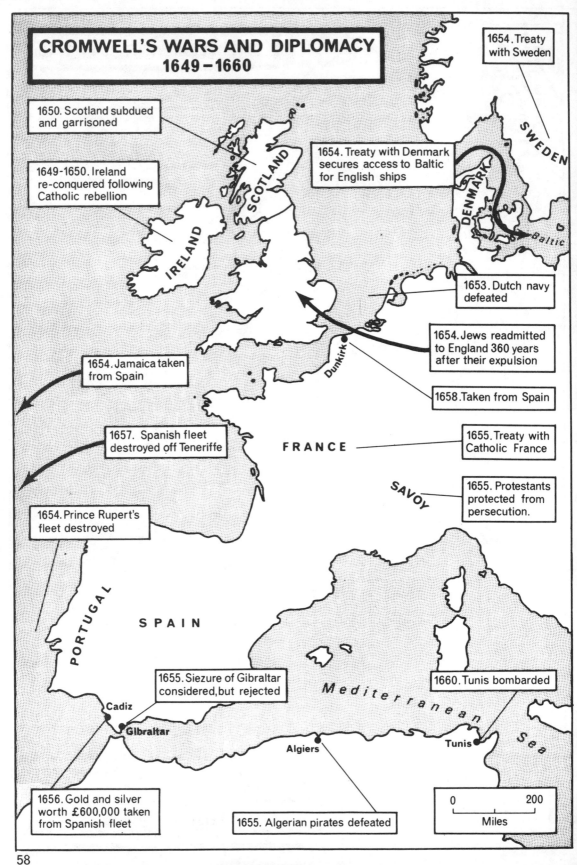

CROMWELL'S WARS AND DIPLOMACY 1649–1660

1650. Scotland subdued and garrisoned

1649-1650. Ireland re-conquered following Catholic rebellion

1654. Treaty with Sweden

1654. Treaty with Denmark secures access to Baltic for English ships

SWEDEN

DENMARK

Baltic

SCOTLAND

IRELAND

1653. Dutch navy defeated

1654. Jamaica taken from Spain

Dunkirk

1654. Jews readmitted to England 360 years after their expulsion

1658. Taken from Spain

1657. Spanish fleet destroyed off Teneriffe

FRANCE

1655. Treaty with Catholic France

SAVOY

1655. Protestants protected from persecution.

1654. Prince Rupert's fleet destroyed

PORTUGAL

SPAIN

1655. Siezure of Gibraltar considered, but rejected

Mediterranean Sea

1660. Tunis bombarded

Cadiz

Gibraltar

Algiers

Tunis

1656. Gold and silver worth £600,000 taken from Spanish fleet

1655. Algerian pirates defeated

0   200
Miles

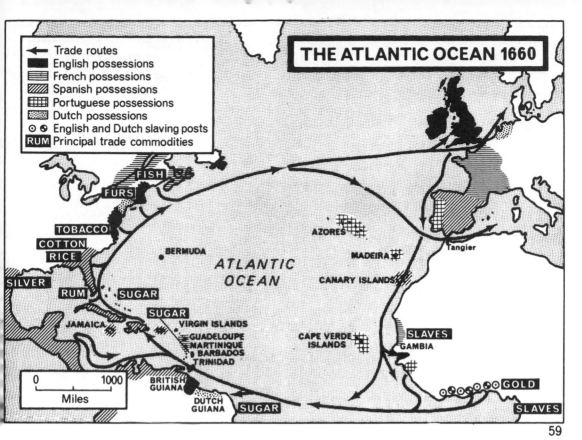

THE ATLANTIC OCEAN 1660

Trade routes
English possessions
French possessions
Spanish possessions
Portuguese possessions
Dutch possessions
English and Dutch slaving posts
RUM Principal trade commodities

FISH
FURS
TOBACCO
COTTON
RICE
SILVER
RUM
SUGAR
SUGAR
JAMAICA
SUGAR
VIRGIN ISLANDS
GUADELOUPE
MARTINIQUE
BARBADOS
TRINIDAD
BRITISH GUIANA
DUTCH GUIANA
SUGAR
BERMUDA
ATLANTIC OCEAN
AZORES
MADEIRA
CANARY ISLANDS
Tangier
CAPE VERDE ISLANDS
SLAVES
GAMBIA
GOLD
SLAVES

0   1000
Miles

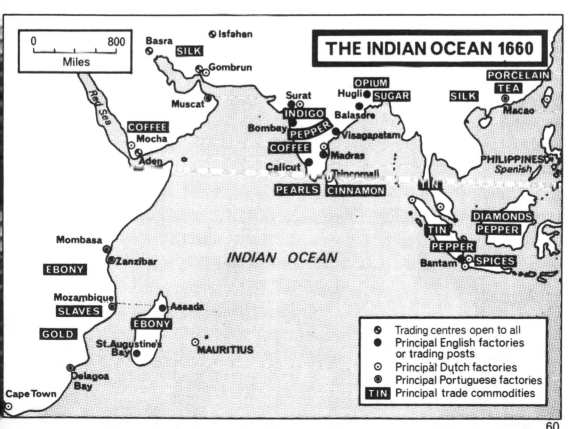

THE INDIAN OCEAN 1660

0   800
Miles

Basra
Isfahan
SILK
Gombrun
Muscat
Red Sea
COFFEE
Mocha
Aden
Surat
INDIGO
Bombay
PEPPER
COFFEE
Calicut
PEARLS
Mombasa
Zanzibar
EBONY
Mozambique
SLAVES
GOLD
Assada
EBONY
St. Augustine's Bay
MAURITIUS
Cape Town
Delagoa Bay

OPIUM
Hugli
SUGAR
Balasore
Visagapatam
Madras
Trincomali
CINNAMON
PORCELAIN
TEA
SILK
Macao
PHILIPPINES
Spanish
TIN
TIN
PEPPER
Bantam
DIAMONDS
PEPPER
SPICES

INDIAN OCEAN

Trading centres open to all
Principal English factories or trading posts
Principal Dutch factories
Principal Portuguese factories
TIN Principal trade commodities

THE THREE DUTCH WARS

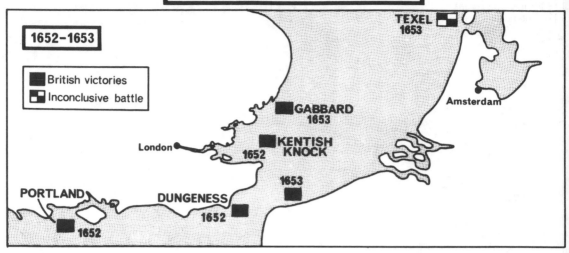

1652-1653

■ British victories
◧ Inconclusive battle

TEXEL
1653

Amsterdam

GABBARD
1653

London
1652

KENTISH
KNOCK

PORTLAND
1652

DUNGENESS
1652

1653

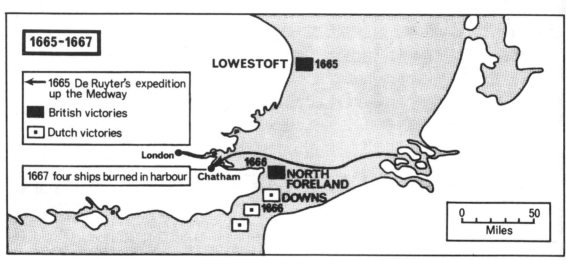

1665-1667

← 1665 De Ruyter's expedition
up the Medway
■ British victories
◱ Dutch victories

LOWESTOFT 1665

London

1667 four ships burned in harbour

Chatham
1666

NORTH
FORELAND
DOWNS
1666

0   50
Miles

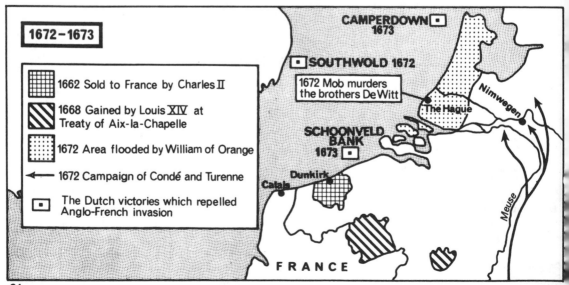

1672-1673

▦ 1662 Sold to France by Charles II

▨ 1668 Gained by Louis XIV at
Treaty of Aix-la-Chapelle

⊡ 1672 Area flooded by William of Orange

← 1672 Campaign of Condé and Turenne

◱ The Dutch victories which repelled
Anglo-French invasion

CAMPERDOWN ◱
1673

◱ SOUTHWOLD 1672

1672 Mob murders
the brothers De Witt

Nimwegen

The Hague

SCHOONVELD
BANK
1673 ◱

Dunkirk

Calais

Meuse

FRANCE

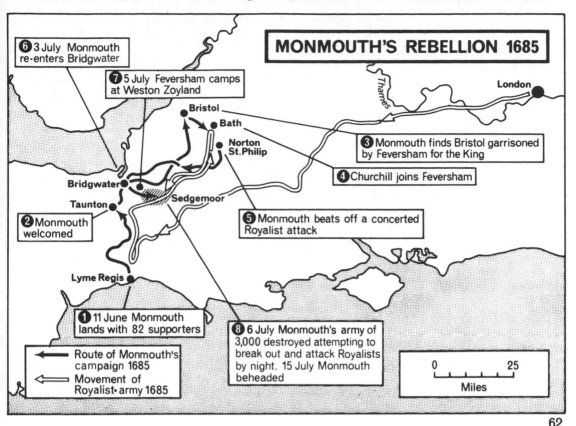

MONMOUTH'S REBELLION 1685

6 3 July Monmouth re-enters Bridgwater

7 5 July Feversham camps at Weston Zoyland

3 Monmouth finds Bristol garrisoned by Feversham for the King

4 Churchill joins Feversham

5 Monmouth beats off a concerted Royalist attack

2 Monmouth welcomed

1 11 June Monmouth lands with 82 supporters

8 6 July Monmouth's army of 3,000 destroyed attempting to break out and attack Royalists by night. 15 July Monmouth beheaded

London

Thames

Bristol

Bath

Norton St.Philip

Bridgwater

Taunton

Sedgemoor

Lyme Regis

→ Route of Monmouth's campaign 1685
⇨ Movement of Royalist army 1685

0 — 25 Miles

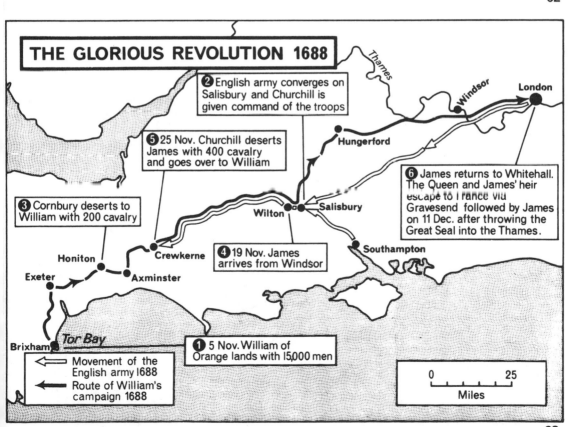

THE GLORIOUS REVOLUTION 1688

2 English army converges on Salisbury and Churchill is given command of the troops

5 25 Nov. Churchill deserts James with 400 cavalry and goes over to William

3 Cornbury deserts to William with 200 cavalry

6 James returns to Whitehall. The Queen and James' heir escape to France via Gravesend followed by James on 11 Dec. after throwing the Great Seal into the Thames.

4 19 Nov. James arrives from Windsor

1 5 Nov. William of Orange lands with 15,000 men

Thames

Windsor

London

Hungerford

Wilton

Salisbury

Southampton

Honiton

Crewkerne

Exeter

Axminster

Brixham

Tor Bay

⇨ Movement of the English army 1688
→ Route of William's campaign 1688

0 — 25 Miles

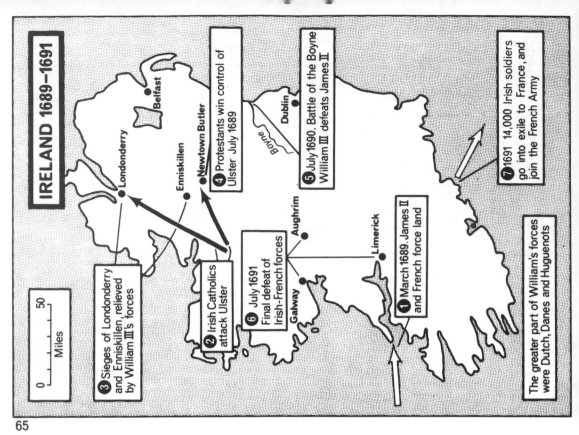

IRELAND 1689–1691

Miles 0 — 50

Belfast

Londonderry

Enniskillen

● Newtown Butler

④ Protestants win control of Ulster July 1689

Dublin

Boyne

⑤ July 1690. Battle of the Boyne William III defeats James II

③ Sieges of Londonderry and Enniskillen, relieved by William III's forces

② Irish Catholics attack Ulster

Aughrim

Galway

Limerick

⑥ July 1691 Final defeat of Irish-French forces

① March 1689. James II and French force land

⑦ 1691 14,000 Irish soldiers go into exile to France, and join the French Army

The greater part of William's forces were Dutch, Danes and Huguenots

65

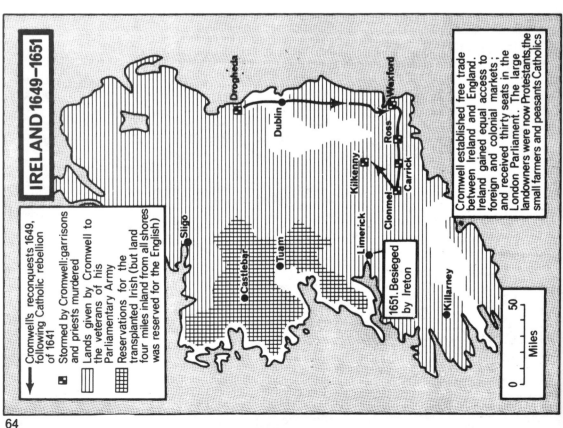

IRELAND 1649–1651

Drogheda

Dublin

Wexford

Ross

Carrick

Clonmel

Kilkenny

Limerick

Sligo

Castlebar

Tuam

1651. Besieged by Ireton

Killarney

→ Cromwell's reconquests 1649, following Catholic rebellion of 1641

■ Stormed by Cromwell; garrisons and priests murdered

▥ Lands given by Cromwell to the veterans of his Parliamentary Army

▦ Reservations for the transplanted Irish (but land four miles inland from all shores was reserved for the English)

Cromwell established free trade between Ireland and England. Ireland gained equal access to foreign and colonial markets; and received thirty seats in the London Parliament. The large landowners were now Protestants, the small farmers and peasants Catholics.

Miles 0 — 50

64

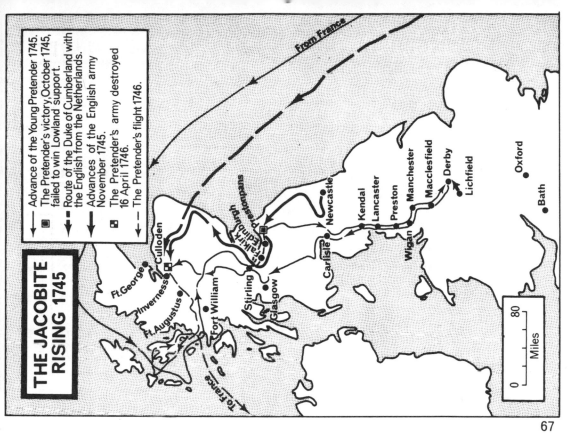

THE JACOBITE RISING 1745

Advance of the Young Pretender 1745.

The Pretender's victory, October 1745, failed to win Lowland support.

Route of the Duke of Cumberland with the English from the Netherlands.

Advances of the English army November 1745.

The Pretender's army destroyed 16 April 1746.

The Pretender's flight 1746.

From France

To France

Ft.George
Culloden
Inverness
Ft.Augustus
Fort William
Stirling
Glasgow
Edinburgh
Falkirk
Prestonpans
Carlisle
Newcastle
Kendal
Lancaster
Preston
Wigan
Manchester
Macclesfield
Derby
Lichfield
Oxford
Bath

0   80
Miles

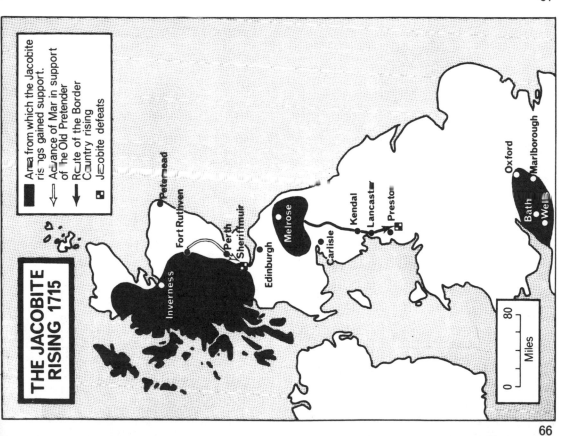

THE JACOBITE RISING 1715

Area from which the Jacobite risings gained support.

Advance of Mar in support of the Old Pretender

Route of the Border Country rising

Jacobite defeats

Peterhead
Fort Ruthven
Inverness
Perth
Sheriffmuir
Edinburgh
Melrose
Carlisle
Kendal
Lancaster
Preston
Oxford
Marlborough
Bath
Wells

0   80
Miles

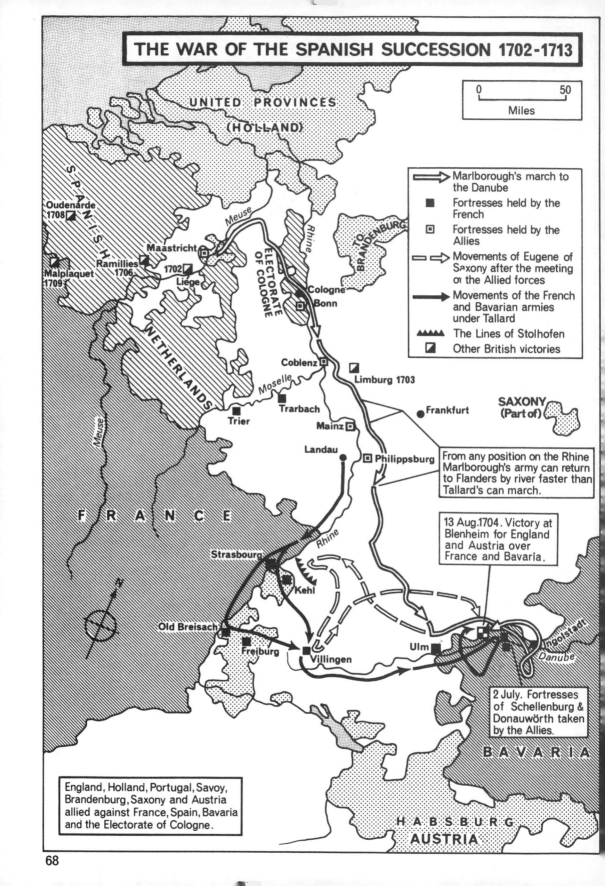

THE WAR OF THE SPANISH SUCCESSION 1702-1713

UNITED PROVINCES
(HOLLAND)

0 — 50
Miles

TO BRANDENBURG

S P A N I S H

Oudenarde 1708

Maastricht

Ramillies 1706

1702

Malplaquet 1709

Liège

N E T H E R L A N D S

ELECTORATE OF COLOGNE

Rhine

Cologne
Bonn

Meuse

Coblenz

Limburg 1703

Moselle

Trarbach

Trier

Mainz

Landau

Philippsburg

Frankfurt

SAXONY
(Part of)

From any position on the Rhine Marlborough's army can return to Flanders by river faster than Tallard's can march.

F R A N C E

Meuse

Rhine

Strasbourg

Kehl

13 Aug.1704. Victory at Blenheim for England and Austria over France and Bavaria.

Old Breisach

Freiburg

Villingen

Ulm

Ingolstadt

Danube

2 July. Fortresses of Schellenburg & Donauwörth taken by the Allies.

B A V A R I A

England, Holland, Portugal, Savoy, Brandenburg, Saxony and Austria allied against France, Spain, Bavaria and the Electorate of Cologne.

H A B S B U R G
AUSTRIA

Legend:

⇨ Marlborough's march to the Danube

■ Fortresses held by the French

▣ Fortresses held by the Allies

⇨ Movements of Eugene of Saxony after the meeting of the Allied forces

➙ Movements of the French and Bavarian armies under Tallard

▲▲▲▲ The Lines of Stolhofen

◪ Other British victories

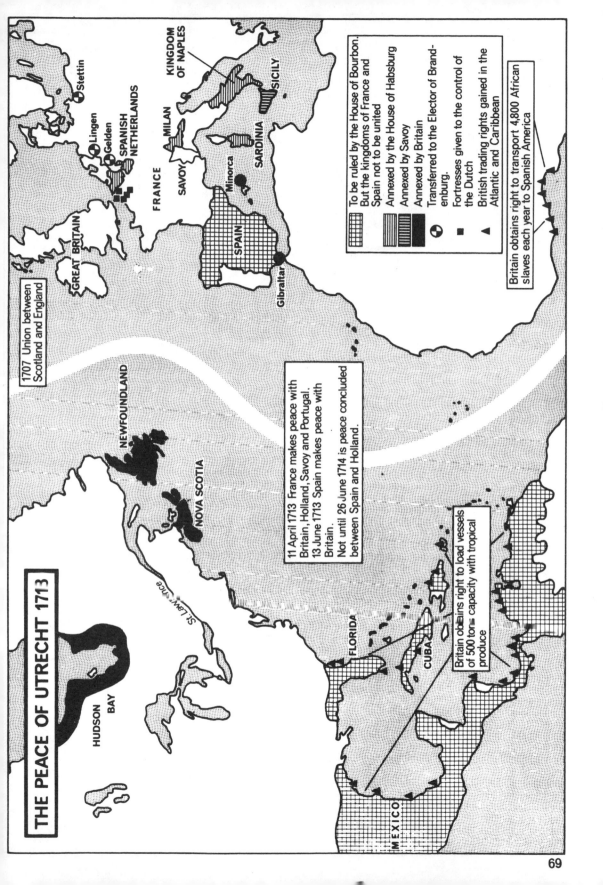

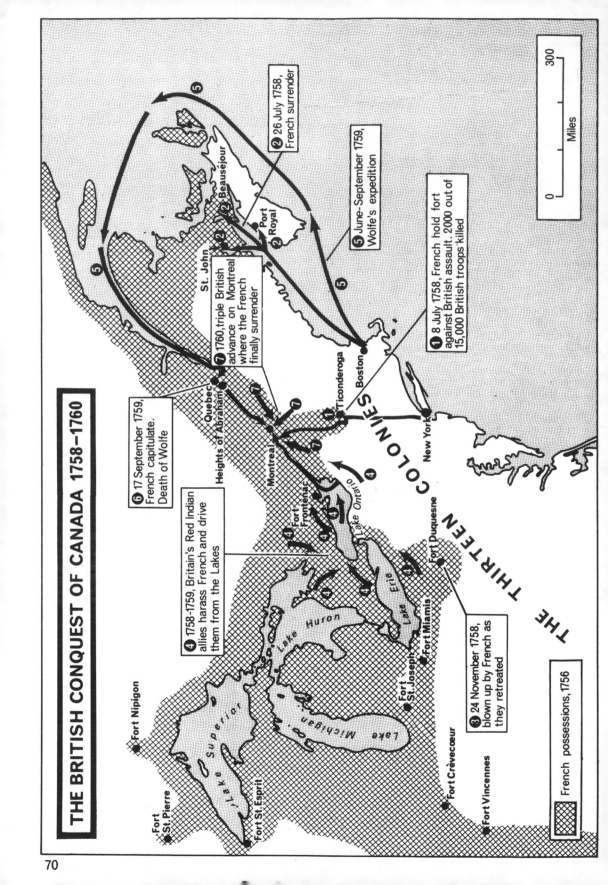

THE BRITISH CONQUEST OF CANADA 1758–1760

2 26 July 1758, French surrender

5 June–September 1759, Wolfe's expedition

1 8 July 1758, French hold fort against British assault. 2000 out of 15,000 British troops killed

7 1760, triple British advance on Montreal where the French finally surrender

6 17 September 1759, French capitulate. Death of Wolfe

4 1758-1759, Britain's Red Indian allies harass French and drive them from the Lakes

3 24 November 1758, blown up by French as they retreated

French possessions, 1756

300

Miles

Port Royal

Beauséjour

St. John

Boston

Ticonderoga

New York

Quebec

Heights of Abraham

Montreal

Fort Frontenac

Lake Ontario

Fort Duquesne

Fort Miamis

Fort St. Joseph

Lake Erie

Lake Huron

Lake Michigan

Lake Superior

Fort Nipigon

Fort St. Pierre

Fort St. Esprit

Fort Crèvecœur

Fort Vincennes

THE THIRTEEN COLONIES

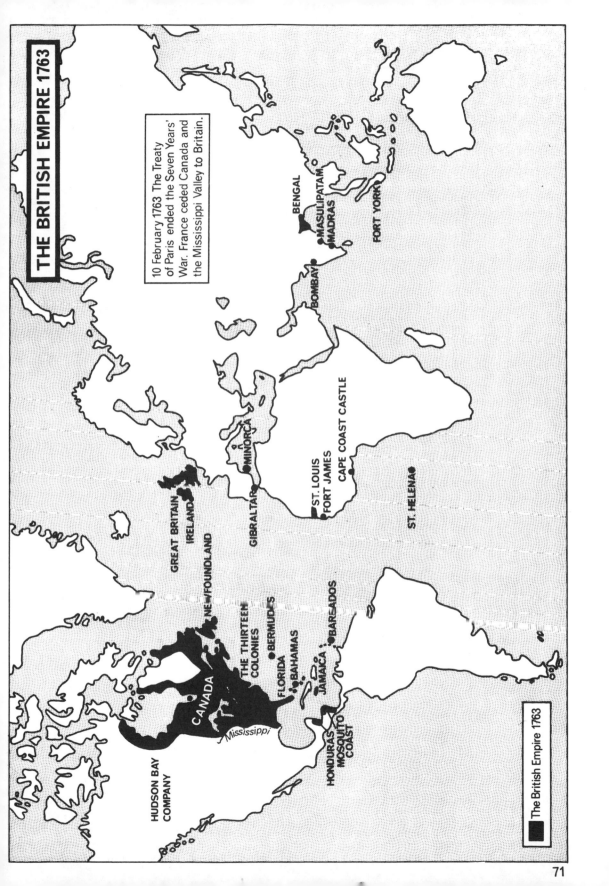

THE BRITISH EMPIRE 1763

10 February 1763 The Treaty of Paris ended the Seven Years' War. France ceded Canada and the Mississippi Valley to Britain.

HUDSON BAY COMPANY

CANADA

Mississippi

NEWFOUNDLAND

THE THIRTEEN COLONIES

FLORIDA

BERMUDAS

BAHAMAS

JAMAICA

BARBADOS

HONDURAS

MOSQUITO COAST

GREAT BRITAIN

IRELAND

GIBRALTAR

MINORCA

ST. LOUIS

FORT JAMES

CAPE COAST CASTLE

ST. HELENA

BENGAL

MASULIPATAM

MADRAS

BOMBAY

FORT YORK

☐ The British Empire 1763

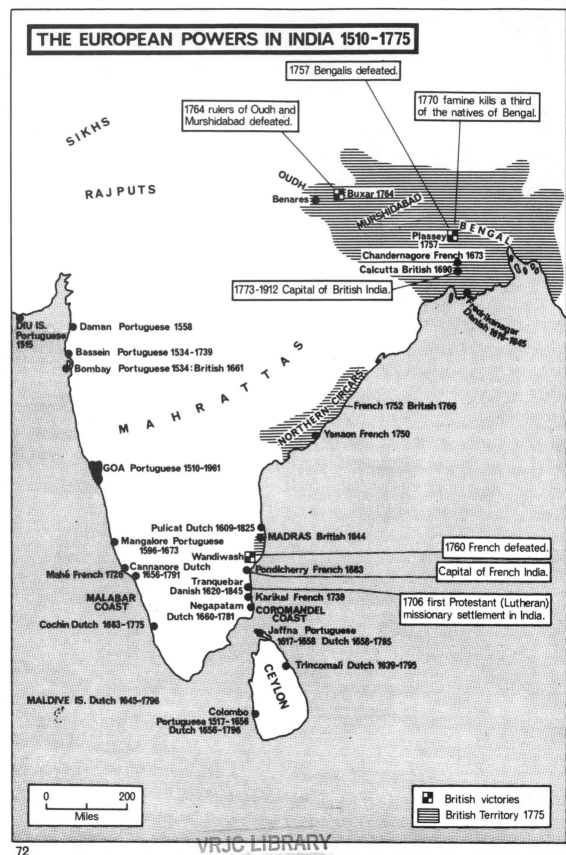

THE EUROPEAN POWERS IN INDIA 1510-1775

1757 Bengalis defeated.

1770 famine kills a third of the natives of Bengal.

1764 rulers of Oudh and Murshidabad defeated.

SIKHS

RAJPUTS

OUDH

Benares

Buxar 1764

MURSHIDABAD

BENGAL

Plassey 1757

Chandernagore French 1673

Calcutta British 1690

1773-1912 Capital of British India.

Danish Serampore Danish 1616-1845

DIU IS. Portuguese 1515

Daman Portuguese 1558

Bassein Portuguese 1534-1739

Bombay Portuguese 1534: British 1661

M A H R A T T A S

NORTHERN CIRCARS

French 1752 British 1766

Yanaon French 1750

GOA Portuguese 1510-1961

Pulicat Dutch 1609-1825

Mangalore Portuguese 1596-1673

Mahé French 1726

Cannanore Dutch 1656-1791

MADRAS British 1644

Wandiwash

Pondicherry French 1683

Tranquebar Danish 1620-1845

Karikal French 1739

Negapatam Dutch 1660-1781

MALABAR COAST

Cochin Dutch 1663-1775

COROMANDEL COAST

Jaffna Portuguese 1617-1658 Dutch 1658-1795

1760 French defeated.

Capital of French India.

1706 first Protestant (Lutheran) missionary settlement in India.

Trincomali Dutch 1639-1795

MALDIVE IS. Dutch 1945-1796

CEYLON

Colombo Portuguese 1517-1656 Dutch 1656-1796

▣	British victories
☰	British Territory 1775

0   200
Miles

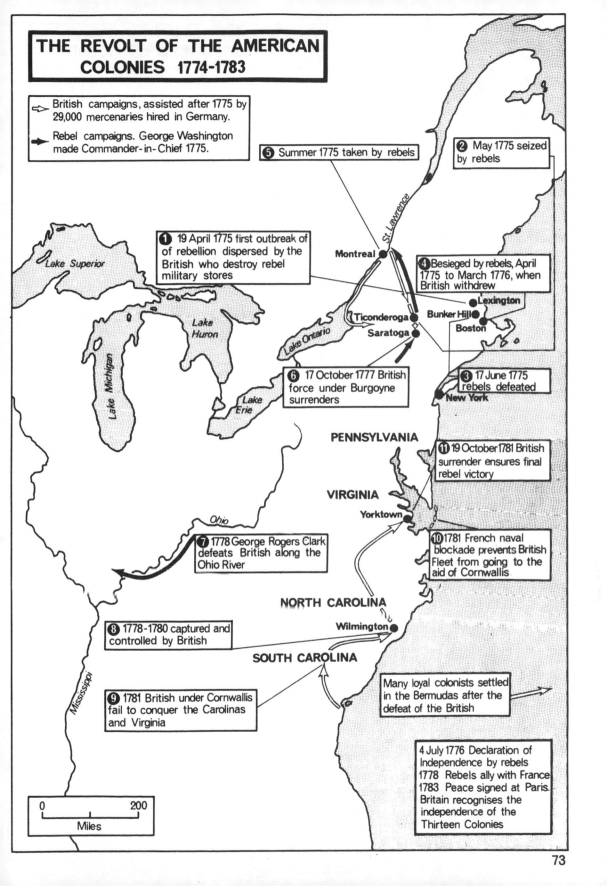

THE REVOLT OF THE AMERICAN COLONIES 1774-1783

⇨ British campaigns, assisted after 1775 by 29,000 mercenaries hired in Germany.

➡ Rebel campaigns. George Washington made Commander-in-Chief 1775.

5 Summer 1775 taken by rebels

2 May 1775 seized by rebels

1 19 April 1775 first outbreak of of rebellion dispersed by the British who destroy rebel military stores

4 Besieged by rebels, April 1775 to March 1776, when British withdrew

Montreal

Lexington
Bunker Hill
Boston

Lake Superior

Lake Huron

Lake Michigan

Lake Ontario

Ticonderoga

Saratoga

Lake Erie

6 17 October 1777 British force under Burgoyne surrenders

3 17 June 1775 rebels defeated

New York

PENNSYLVANIA

11 19 October 1781 British surrender ensures final rebel victory

VIRGINIA

Ohio

Yorktown

7 1778 George Rogers Clark defeats British along the Ohio River

10 1781 French naval blockade prevents British Fleet from going to the aid of Cornwallis.

NORTH CAROLINA

8 1778-1780 captured and controlled by British

Wilmington

SOUTH CAROLINA

Mississippi

Many loyal colonists settled in the Bermudas after the defeat of the British

9 1781 British under Cornwallis fail to conquer the Carolinas and Virginia

4 July 1776 Declaration of Independence by rebels 1778 Rebels ally with France 1783 Peace signed at Paris. Britain recognises the independence of the Thirteen Colonies

0   200
Miles

73

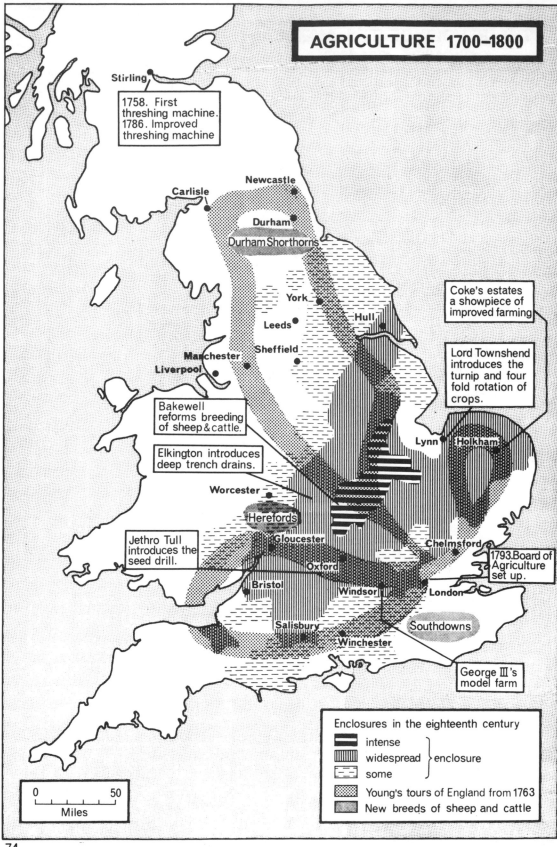

AGRICULTURE 1700–1800

Stirling

1758. First
threshing machine.
1786. Improved
threshing machine

Carlisle

Newcastle

Durham

Durham Shorthorns

York

Leeds

Hull

Sheffield

Manchester

Liverpool

Coke's estates
a showpiece of
improved farming

Lord Townshend
introduces the
turnip and four
fold rotation of
crops.

Bakewell
reforms breeding
of sheep & cattle.

Elkington introduces
deep trench drains.

Lynn

Holkham

Worcester

Herefords

Jethro Tull
introduces the
seed drill.

Gloucester

Oxford

Chelmsford

1793. Board of
Agriculture
set up.

Bristol

Windsor

London

Salisbury

Southdowns

Winchester

George III's
model farm

Enclosures in the eighteenth century

▬▬▬	intense
▥▥▥	widespread } enclosure
- - -	some
▦▦▦	Young's tours of England from 1763
▨▨▨	New breeds of sheep and cattle

0   50
Miles

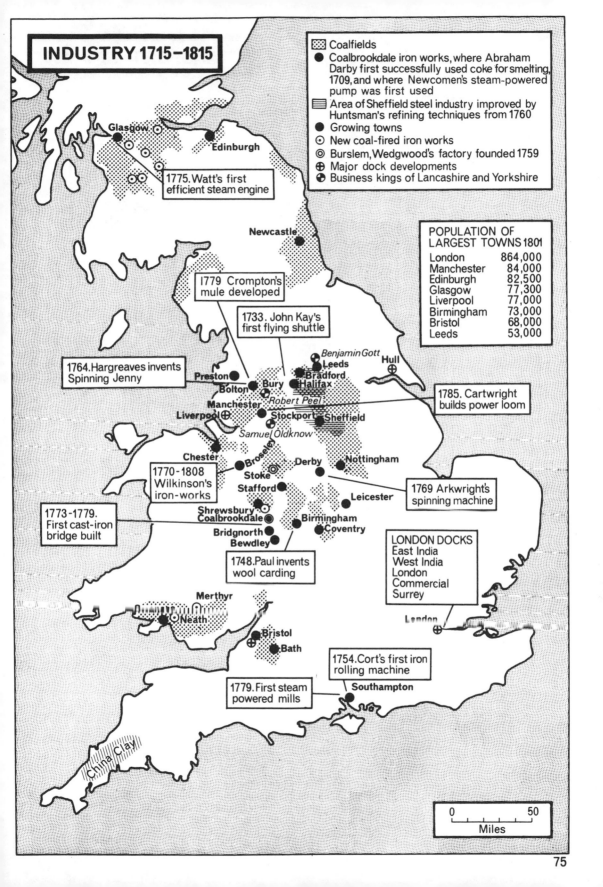

INDUSTRY 1715–1815

Legend:
- ▦ Coalfields
- ● Coalbrookdale iron works, where Abraham Darby first successfully used coke for smelting, 1709, and where Newcomen's steam-powered pump was first used
- ▤ Area of Sheffield steel industry improved by Huntsman's refining techniques from 1760
- ● Growing towns
- ⊙ New coal-fired iron works
- ◎ Burslem, Wedgwood's factory founded 1759
- ⊕ Major dock developments
- ⊕ Business kings of Lancashire and Yorkshire

Glasgow
Edinburgh

1775. Watt's first efficient steam engine

Newcastle

1779 Crompton's mule developed

1733. John Kay's first flying shuttle

1764. Hargreaves invents Spinning Jenny

Benjamin Gott
Leeds
Hull
Preston
Bradford
Bolton   Bury   Halifax
Manchester   Robert Peel
Liverpool   Stockport
Samuel Oldknow   Sheffield

1785. Cartwright builds power loom

Chester   Broseley   Derby   Nottingham
1770–1808 Wilkinson's iron-works
Stoke
Stafford
1773–1779. First cast-iron bridge built
Shrewsbury   Leicester
Coalbrookdale
Birmingham
Bridgnorth   Coventry
Bewdley

1769 Arkwright's spinning machine

1748. Paul invents wool carding

POPULATION OF LARGEST TOWNS 1801

Town	Population
London	864,000
Manchester	84,000
Edinburgh	82,500
Glasgow	77,300
Liverpool	77,000
Birmingham	73,000
Bristol	68,000
Leeds	53,000

LONDON DOCKS
East India
West India
London
Commercial
Surrey

Merthyr
Neath

Bristol
Bath

1754. Cort's first iron rolling machine

1779. First steam powered mills

Southampton

London

China Clay

0   50
Miles

75

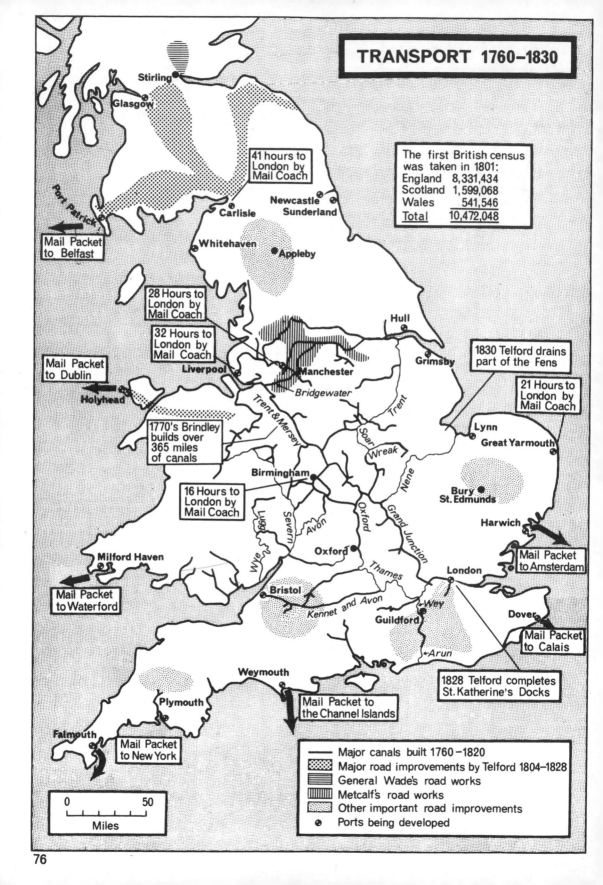

TRANSPORT 1760–1830

Stirling

Glasgow

Port Patrick

Mail Packet to Belfast

41 hours to London by Mail Coach

Carlisle

Newcastle
Sunderland

Whitehaven

Appleby

The first British census was taken in 1801:
England 8,331,434
Scotland 1,599,068
Wales   541,546
Total   10,472,048

28 Hours to London by Mail Coach

Mail Packet to Dublin

32 Hours to London by Mail Coach

Liverpool

Holyhead

Hull

Manchester

Bridgewater

Grimsby

1830 Telford drains part of the Fens

Trent & Mersey

Trent

Lynn

21 Hours to London by Mail Coach

1770's Brindley builds over 365 miles of canals

Soar

Wreak

Great Yarmouth

Birmingham

16 Hours to London by Mail Coach

Lugg

Severn

Avon

Oxford

Nene

Grand Junction

Bury St. Edmunds

Harwich

Mail Packet to Amsterdam

Wye

Oxford

Thames

London

Milford Haven

Mail Packet to Waterford

Bristol

Kennet and Avon

Guildford

Wey

Arun

Dover

Mail Packet to Calais

1828 Telford completes St. Katherine's Docks

Weymouth

Mail Packet to the Channel Islands

Plymouth

Falmouth

Mail Packet to New York

0   50
Miles

—— Major canals built 1760–1820
▨ Major road improvements by Telford 1804–1828
▤ General Wade's road works
▥ Metcalf's road works
▨ Other important road improvements
• Ports being developed

BRITISH EXPANSION IN INDIA 1775-1858

Legend:
- British India 1775.
- Expansion by 1806.
- Expansion by 1836.
- Expansion by 1856.
- ⊕ Main centres of the Indian Mutiny of 1857

Peshawar

PUNJAB

ROHILKHAND   KUMAON

Delhi   Lucknow

Bikaner   DOAB   OUDH   ASSAM

Ajmer   Gwalior

RAJPUTANA   BIHAR   Dacca

SIND   Udaipur   BUNDELKHAND   BENGAL

Indore   Dum   Dum

GUJARAT   Baroda   NAGPUR   Calcutta   ARAKAN

BERAR   Cuttack

Bombay   NIZAM'S   NORTHERN   PEGU
DOMINIONS   CIRCARS

Hyderabad

ANDAMAN ISLANDS

1858 British convict settlement

MYSORE   Madras

**1834 British rule.
1881 Native rajah restored.**

CAFNATIC   TENASSERM.

COCHIN
TRAVANCORE

CEYLON

1815 British sovereignty.

MALDIVE ISLANDS

1796 British.

```
0                    400
        Miles
```

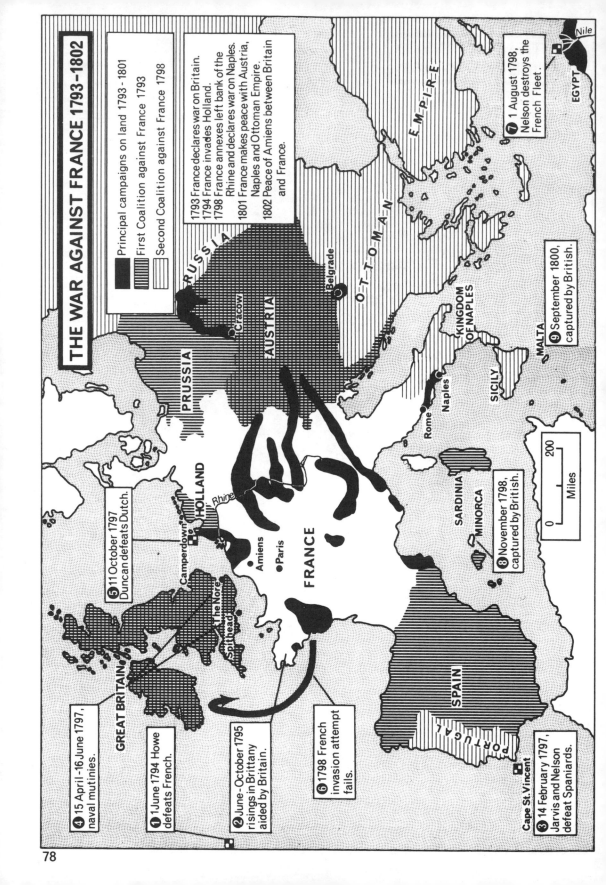

THE WAR AGAINST FRANCE 1793–1802

Principal campaigns on land 1793 - 1801

First Coalition against France 1793

Second Coalition against France 1798

1793 France declares war on Britain.
1794 France invades Holland.
1798 France annexes left bank of the Rhine and declares war on Naples.
1801 France makes peace with Austria, Naples and Ottoman Empire.
1802 Peace of Amiens between Britain and France.

7 1 August 1798, Nelson destroys the French Fleet.

EGYPT

Nile

E M P I R E

O—T—T—O—M—A—N

Belgrade

Cracow

AUSTRIA

PRUSSIA

9 September 1800, captured by British.

KINGDOM OF NAPLES

Naples

Rome

SICILY

MALTA

Rhine

HOLLAND

Camperdown

The Nore

Spithead

GREAT BRITAIN

Amiens

Paris

FRANCE

SARDINIA

MINORCA

8 November 1798, captured by British.

0   200
Miles

5 11 October 1797, Duncan defeats Dutch.

4 15 April -16 June 1797, naval mutinies.

1 1 June 1794 Howe defeats French.

2 June - October 1795 risings in Brittany aided by Britain.

6 1798 French invasion attempt fails.

SPAIN

PORTUGAL

Cape St. Vincent

3 14 February 1797, Jarvis and Nelson defeat Spaniards.

78

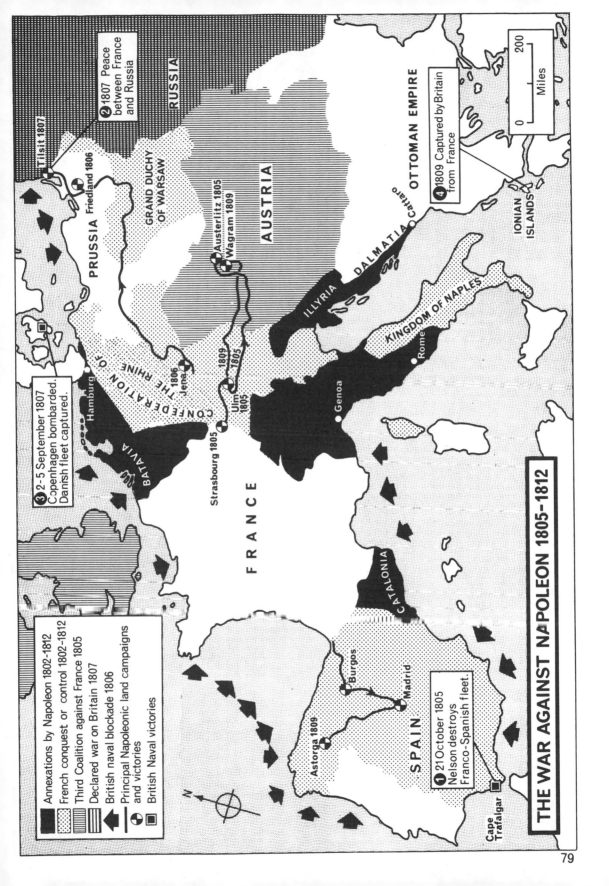

THE WAR AGAINST NAPOLEON 1805–1812

Legend:
- Annexations by Napoleon 1802–1812
- French conquest or control 1802–1812
- Third Coalition against France 1805
- Declared war on Britain 1807
- British naval blockade 1806
- Principal Napoleonic land campaigns and victories
- British Naval victories

① 21 October 1805 Nelson destroys Franco-Spanish fleet.

② 1807 Peace between France and Russia

③ 2–5 September 1807 Copenhagen bombarded. Danish fleet captured.

④ 1809 Captured by Britain from France

RUSSIA

PRUSSIA
Tilsit 1807
Friedland 1806

GRAND DUCHY OF WARSAW

AUSTRIA
Austerlitz 1805
Wagram 1809

CONFEDERATION OF THE RHINE
Hamburg
Jena 1806
Ulm 1805
1809
1805
Strasbourg 1805

BATAVIA

FRANCE

ILLYRIA
DALMATIA
Cattaro

OTTOMAN EMPIRE

IONIAN ISLANDS

KINGDOM OF NAPLES
Rome
Genoa

CATALONIA

SPAIN
Burgos
Madrid
Astorga 1809
Cape Trafalgar

0 200
Miles

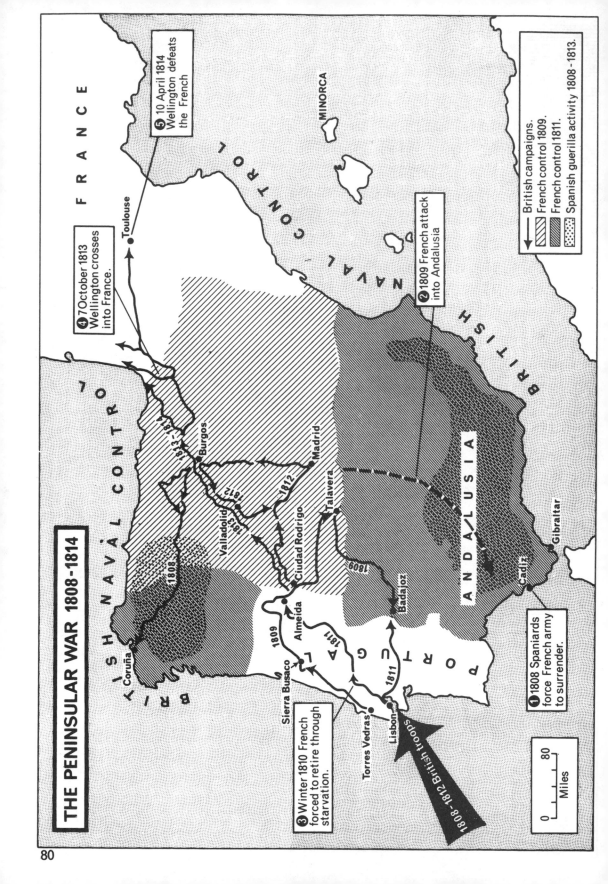

THE PENINSULAR WAR 1808-1814

5 10 April 1814 Wellington defeats the French

4 7 October 1813 Wellington crosses into France.

2 1809 French attack into Andalusia

Legend:
British campaigns.
French control 1809.
French control 1811.
Spanish guerilla activity 1808–1813.

FRANCE

MINORCA

BRITISH NAVAL CONTROL

BRITISH NAVAL CONTROL

Toulouse

Burgos

1813–814

Madrid

Valladolid

1812

1813

1812

Talavera

Ciudad Rodrigo

1809

A N D A L U S I A

Gibraltar

Cadiz

Badajoz

1 1808 Spaniards force French army to surrender.

Almeida

1809

1811

P O R T U G A L

3 Winter 1810 French forced to retire through starvation.

Sierra Busaco

Torres Vedras

Lisbon

1808–1812 British troops

Coruña

0   80
Miles

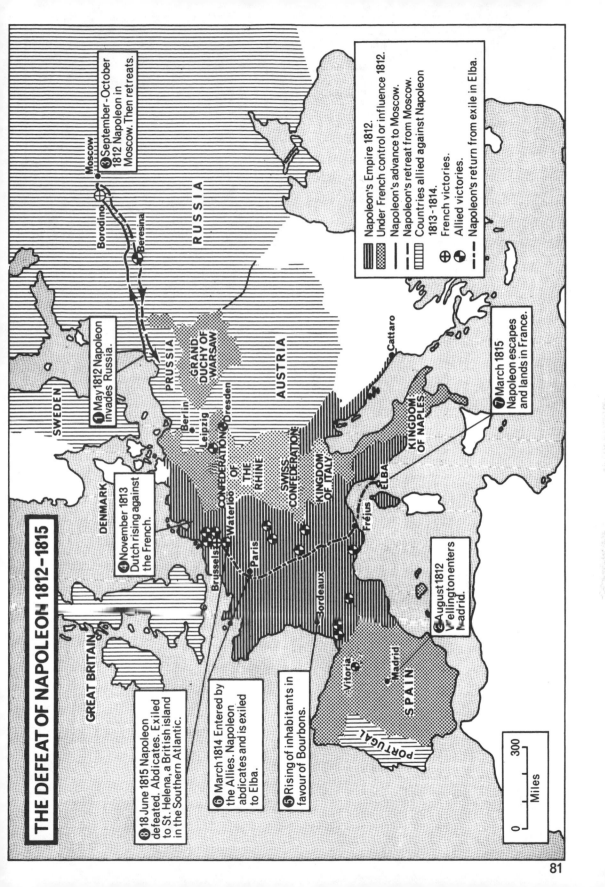

THE DEFEAT OF NAPOLEON 1812–1815

① May 1812 Napoleon invades Russia.

② September - October 1812 Napoleon in Moscow. Then retreats.

④ November 1813 Dutch rising against the French.

⑧ 18 June 1815 Napoleon defeated. Abdicates. Exiled to St. Helena, a British island in the Southern Atlantic.

⑥ March 1814 Entered by the Allies. Napoleon abdicates and is exiled to Elba.

⑤ Rising of inhabitants in favour of Bourbons.

⑦ March 1815 Napoleon escapes and lands in France.

③ August 1812 Wellington enters Madrid.

Key:
- Napoleon's Empire 1812.
- Under French control or influence 1812.
- Napoleon's advance to Moscow.
- Napoleon's retreat from Moscow.
- Countries allied against Napoleon 1813-1814.
- French victories.
- Allied victories.
- Napoleon's return from exile in Elba.

GREAT BRITAIN

SWEDEN

DENMARK

RUSSIA

Moscow
Borodino
Beresina

PRUSSIA

GRAND DUCHY OF WARSAW

Berlin
Leipzig
Dresden

CONFEDERATION OF THE RHINE

AUSTRIA

Waterloo
Brussels
Paris
Bordeaux

SWISS CONFEDERATION

KINGDOM OF ITALY

Fréjus
ELBA

KINGDOM OF NAPLES

Cattaro

SPAIN
Madrid
Vitoria

PORTUGAL

0   300
Miles

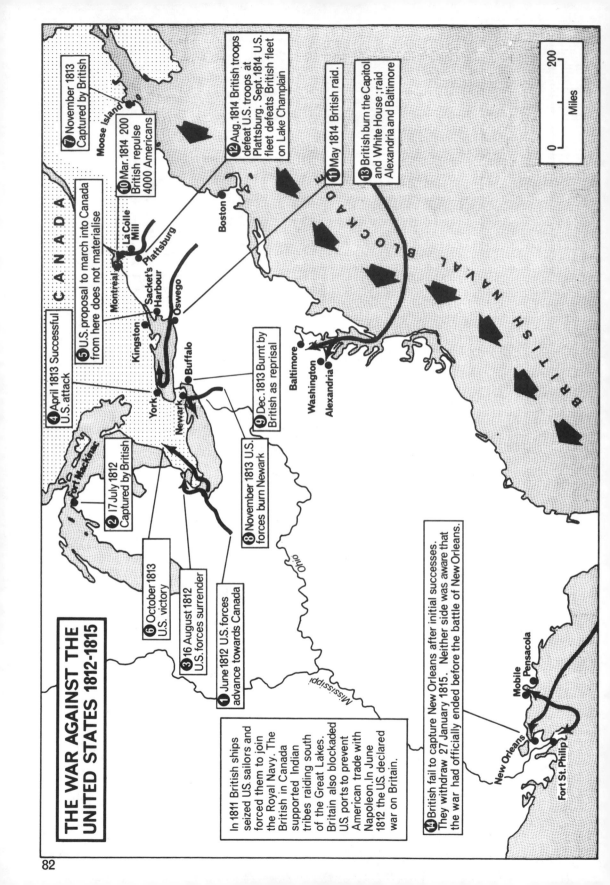

THE WAR AGAINST THE UNITED STATES 1812-1815

CANADA

Moose Island

⑦ November 1813 Captured by British

⑩ Mar. 1814 200 British repulse 4000 Americans

La Colle Mill

⑤ U.S. proposal to march into Canada from here does not materialise

⑫ Aug. 1814 British troops defeat U.S. troops at Plattsburg. Sept. 1814 U.S. fleet defeats British fleet on Lake Champlain

⑪ May 1814 British raid.

⑬ British burn the Capitol and White House; raid Alexandria and Baltimore

Boston

Plattsburg

Montreal

Sacket's Harbour

Kingston

Oswego

④ April 1813 Successful U.S. attack

York

Newark

Buffalo

② 17 July 1812 Captured by British

Fort Mackinac

⑨ Dec. 1813 Burnt by British as reprisal

Baltimore

Washington

Alexandria

BRITISH NAVAL BLOCKADE

⑥ October 1813 U.S. victory

③ 16 August 1812 U.S. forces surrender

⑧ November 1813 U.S. forces burn Newark

① June 1812 U.S. forces advance towards Canada

Ohio

Mississippi

In 1811 British ships seized U.S. sailors and forced them to join the Royal Navy. The British in Canada supported Indian tribes raiding south of the Great Lakes. Britain also blockaded U.S. ports to prevent American trade with Napoleon. In June 1812 the U.S. declared war on Britain.

⑭ British fail to capture New Orleans after initial successes. They withdraw 27 January 1815. Neither side was aware that the war had officially ended before the battle of New Orleans.

Mobile

Pensacola

New Orleans

Fort St. Philip

0 — 200

Miles

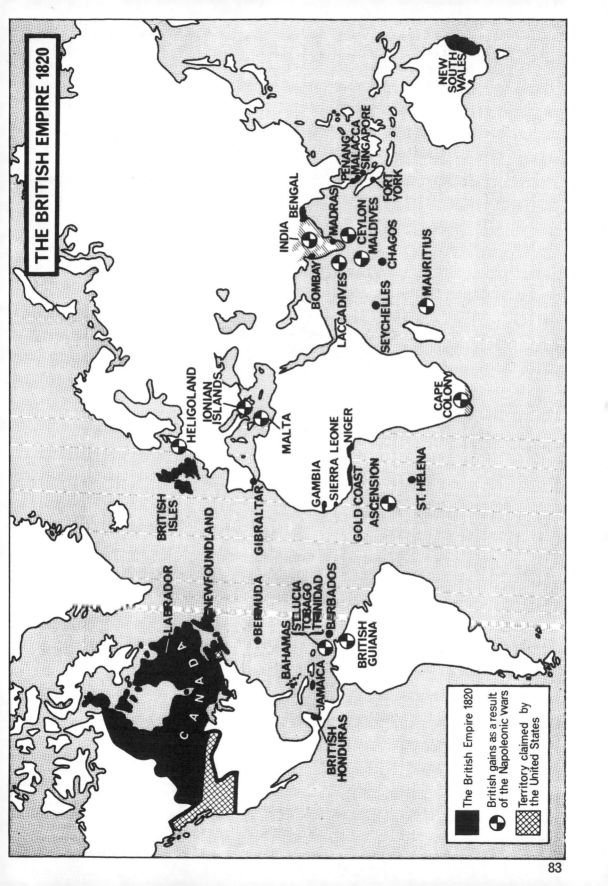

THE BRITISH EMPIRE 1820

NEW SOUTH WALES

PENANG
MALACCA
SINGAPORE

INDIA
BENGAL
MADRAS
CEYLON
MALDIVES
CHAGOS
FORT YORK

BOMBAY
LACCADIVES
SEYCHELLES
MAURITIUS

HELIGOLAND
IONIAN ISLANDS
MALTA

CAPE COLONY

GAMBIA
SIERRA LEONE
NIGER
GOLD COAST
ASCENSION
ST. HELENA

BRITISH ISLES
NEWFOUNDLAND
GIBRALTAR

LABRADOR

BERMUDA
ST. LUCIA
TOBAGO
TRINIDAD
BARBADOS
BAHAMAS
JAMAICA
BRITISH GUIANA
BRITISH HONDURAS

CANADA

The British Empire 1820

British gains as a result
of the Napoleonic wars

Territory claimed by
the United States

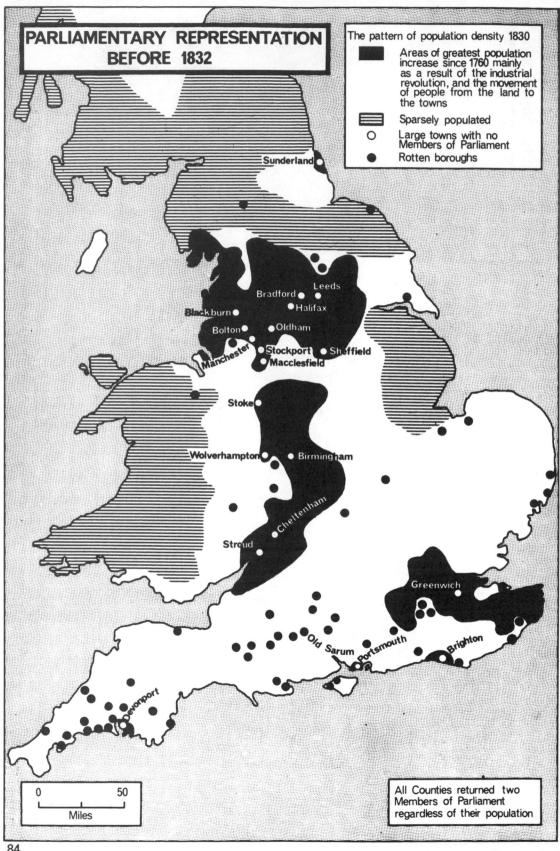

PARLIAMENTARY REPRESENTATION BEFORE 1832

The pattern of population density 1830

Areas of greatest population increase since 1760 mainly as a result of the industrial revolution, and the movement of people from the land to the towns

Sparsely populated

○ Large towns with no Members of Parliament

● Rotten boroughs

Sunderland

Leeds
Bradford
Halifax
Blackburn
Bolton
Oldham
Stockport
Sheffield
Manchester
Macclesfield

Stoke

Wolverhampton
Birmingham

Cheltenham
Stroud

Greenwich

Old Sarum
Portsmouth
Brighton

Devonport

0   50
Miles

All Counties returned two Members of Parliament regardless of their population

84

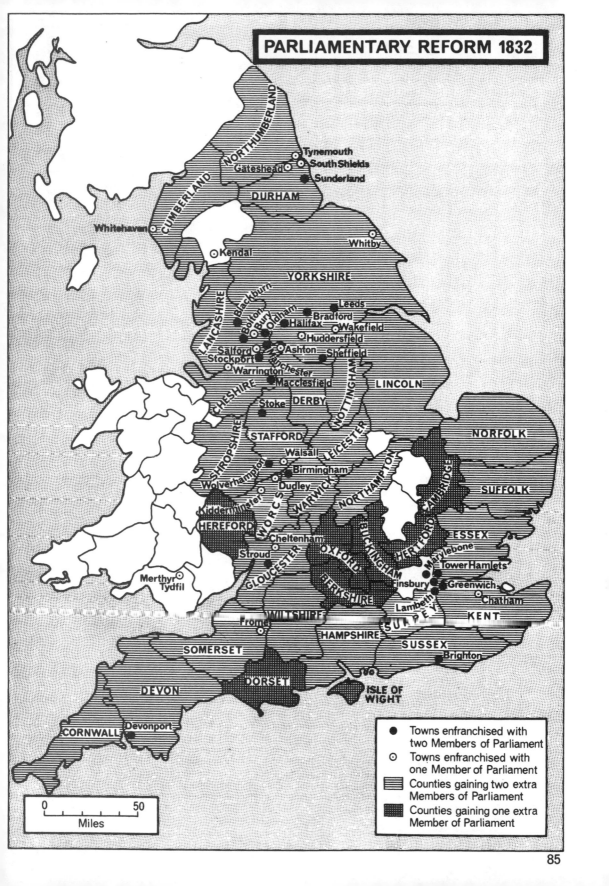

PARLIAMENTARY REFORM 1832

NORTHUMBERLAND

Tynemouth
Gateshead · South Shields
· Sunderland

CUMBERLAND

DURHAM

Whitehaven

Kendal

Whitby

YORKSHIRE

LANCASHIRE

Blackburn
Bolton · Oldham · Leeds
Bury · Bradford
Halifax · Wakefield
Huddersfield
Salford · Ashton
Stockport · Manchester · Sheffield
Warrington
Macclesfield

CHESHIRE

Stoke

DERBY

SHROPSHIRE

STAFFORD

NOTTINGHAM

LINCOLN

NORFOLK

Walsall

Wolverhampton
Kidderminster · Birmingham
Dudley

LEICESTER

NORTHAMPTON

SUFFOLK

WORCS

WARWICK

HEREFORD

Cheltenham

GLOUCESTER

Stroud

Merthyr
Tydfil

OXFORD

BUCKINGHAM

CAMBRIDGE

HERTFORD

ESSEX

Marylebone
Tower Hamlets
Finsbury · Greenwich
Lambeth · Chatham

BERKSHIRE

SURREY

KENT

Frome

WILTSHIRE

HAMPSHIRE

SUSSEX

Brighton

SOMERSET

DORSET

ISLE OF
WIGHT

DEVON

CORNWALL

Devonport

● Towns enfranchised with
   two Members of Parliament

◉ Towns enfranchised with
   one Member of Parliament

Counties gaining two extra
Members of Parliament

Counties gaining one extra
Member of Parliament

0   50
Miles

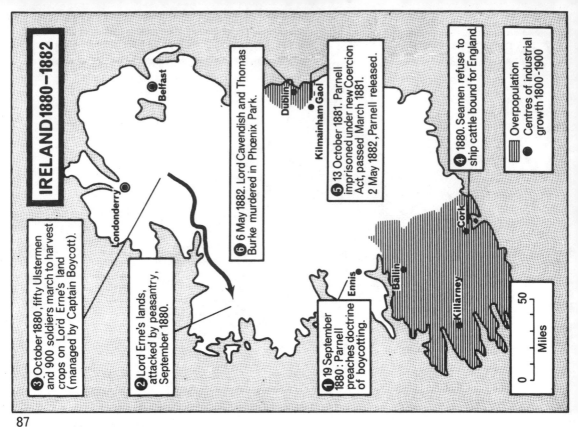

IRELAND 1880–1882

③ October 1880, fifty Ulstermen and 900 soldiers march to harvest crops on Lord Erne's land (managed by Captain Boycott).

② Lord Erne's lands, attacked by peasantry, September 1880.

⑥ 6 May 1882. Lord Cavendish and Thomas Burke murdered in Phoenix Park.

⑤ 13 October 1881. Parnell imprisoned under new Coercion Act, passed March 1881. 2 May 1882, Parnell released.

④ 1880. Seamen refuse to ship cattle bound for England.

① 19 September 1880 : Parnell preaches doctrine of boycotting.

Belfast

Londonderry

Dublin

Kilmainham Gaol

Ennis

Ballin

Killarney

Cork

- ▤ Overpopulation
- ● Centres of industrial growth 1800 -1900

0 50
Miles

87

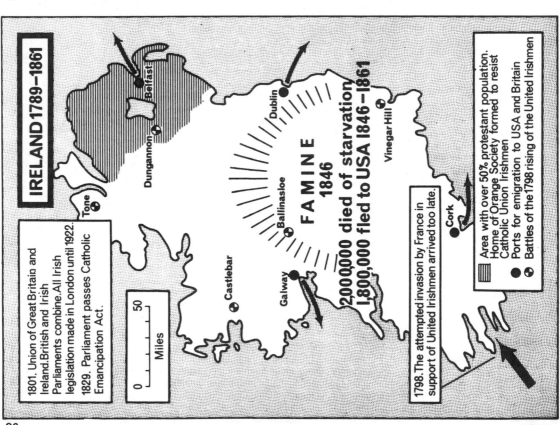

IRELAND 1789–1861

1801. Union of Great Britain and Ireland. British and Irish Parliaments combine. All Irish legislation made in London until 1922.

1829. Parliament passes Catholic Emancipation Act.

Tone

Castlebar

Dungannon

Belfast

Dublin

Galway

Ballinasloe

F A M I N E 1846

2,000,000 died of starvation
1,800,000 fled to USA 1846–1861

Vinegar Hill

Cork

1798. The attempted invasion by France in support of United Irishmen arrived too late.

- ▤ Area with over 50% protestant population. Home of Orange Society formed to resist Catholic Union Irishmen
- ● Ports for emigration to USA and Britain
- ✠ Battles of the 1798 rising of the United Irishmen

0 50
Miles

86

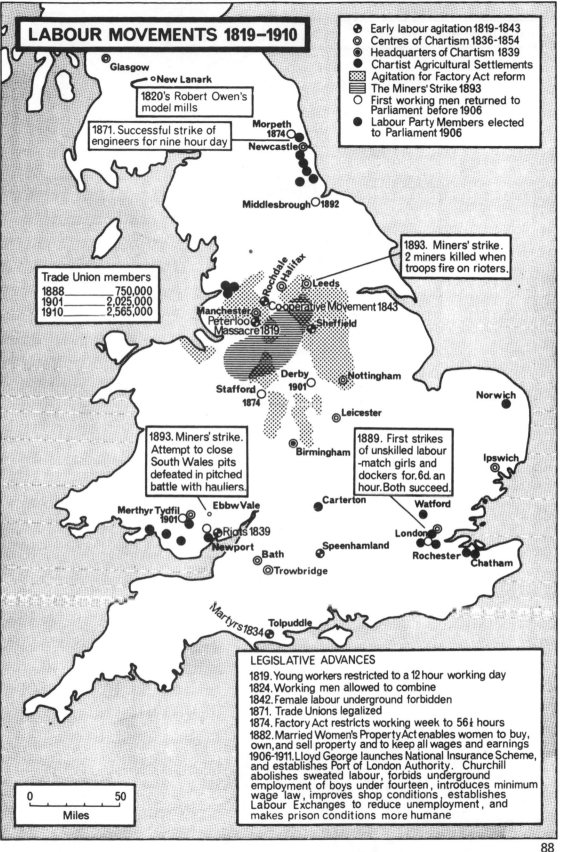

LABOUR MOVEMENTS 1819–1910

Legend:
- Early labour agitation 1819-1843
- Centres of Chartism 1836-1854
- Headquarters of Chartism 1839
- Chartist Agricultural Settlements
- Agitation for Factory Act reform
- The Miners' Strike 1893
- First working men returned to Parliament before 1906
- Labour Party Members elected to Parliament 1906

Glasgow

New Lanark

1820's Robert Owen's model mills

1871. Successful strike of engineers for nine hour day

Morpeth 1874

Newcastle

Middlesbrough 1892

1893. Miners' strike. 2 miners killed when troops fire on rioters.

Rochdale
Halifax
Leeds

Trade Union members
1888 ———— 750,000
1901 ———— 2,025,000
1910 ———— 2,565,000

Manchester
Cooperative Movement 1843
Peterloo Massacre 1819
Sheffield

Derby 1901

Nottingham

Stafford 1874

Norwich

Leicester

1893. Miners' strike. Attempt to close South Wales pits defeated in pitched battle with hauliers.

Birmingham

1889. First strikes of unskilled labour -match girls and dockers for.6d. an hour.Both succeed.

Ipswich

Merthyr Tydfil 1901

Ebbw Vale

Riots 1839

Newport

Bath

Trowbridge

Carterton

Speenhamland

Watford

London

Rochester

Chatham

Martyrs 1834   Tolpuddle

LEGISLATIVE ADVANCES
1819. Young workers restricted to a 12 hour working day
1824. Working men allowed to combine
1842. Female labour underground forbidden
1871. Trade Unions legalized
1874. Factory Act restricts working week to 56½ hours
1882. Married Women's Property Act enables women to buy, own, and sell property and to keep all wages and earnings
1906-1911. Lloyd George launches National Insurance Scheme, and establishes Port of London Authority. Churchill abolishes sweated labour, forbids underground employment of boys under fourteen, introduces minimum wage law, improves shop conditions, establishes Labour Exchanges to reduce unemployment, and makes prison conditions more humane

0   50
Miles

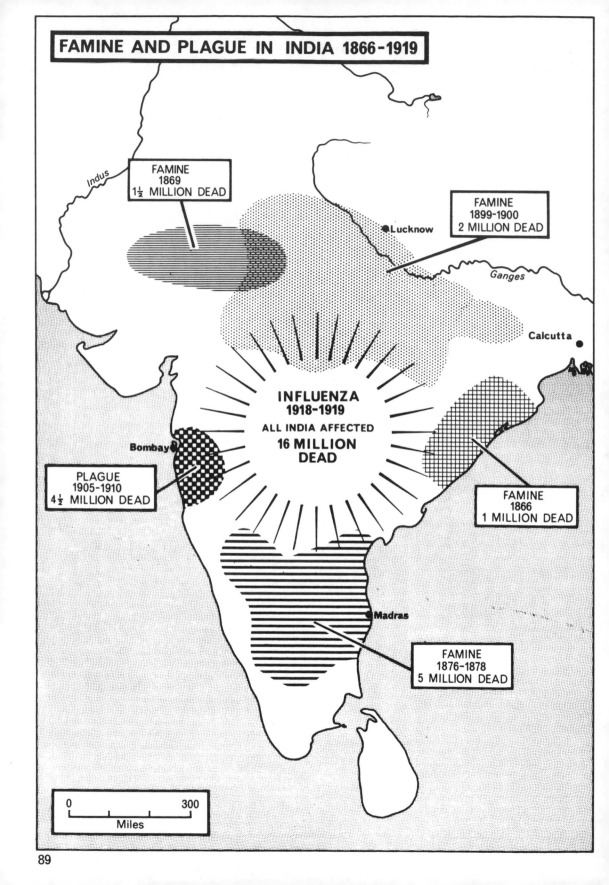

FAMINE AND PLAGUE IN INDIA 1866-1919

FAMINE
1869
1½ MILLION DEAD

FAMINE
1899-1900
2 MILLION DEAD

●Lucknow

Indus

Ganges

●Calcutta

Bombay●

PLAGUE
1905-1910
4½ MILLION DEAD

INFLUENZA
1918-1919
ALL INDIA AFFECTED
16 MILLION
DEAD

FAMINE
1866
1 MILLION DEAD

●Madras

FAMINE
1876-1878
5 MILLION DEAD

0   300
Miles

89

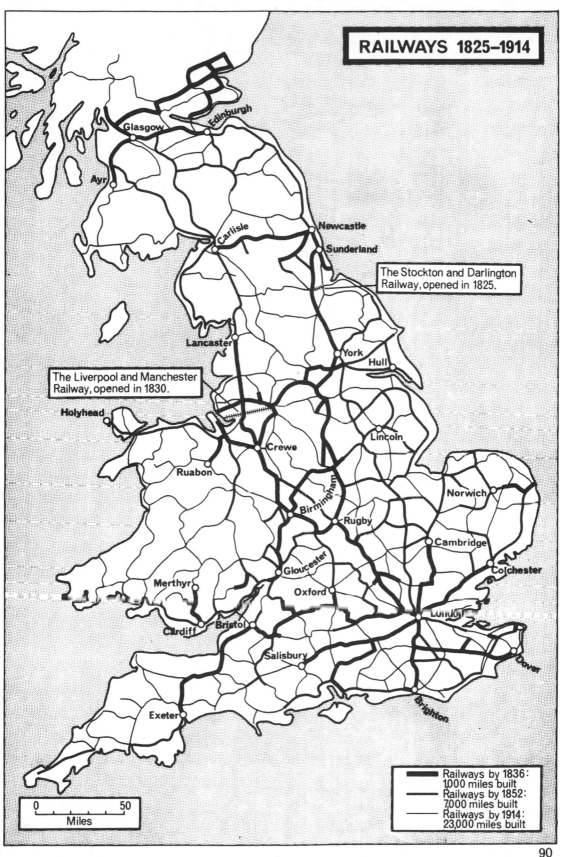

RAILWAYS 1825–1914

The Stockton and Darlington Railway, opened in 1825.

The Liverpool and Manchester Railway, opened in 1830.

Glasgow
Edinburgh
Ayr
Carlisle
Newcastle
Sunderland
Lancaster
York
Hull
Holyhead
Crewe
Lincoln
Ruabon
Birmingham
Norwich
Rugby
Cambridge
Gloucester
Colchester
Merthyr
Oxford
Cardiff
Bristol
London
Salisbury
Dover
Brighton
Exeter

	Railways by 1836: 1000 miles built
	Railways by 1852: 7,000 miles built
	Railways by 1914: 23,000 miles built

0   50
Miles

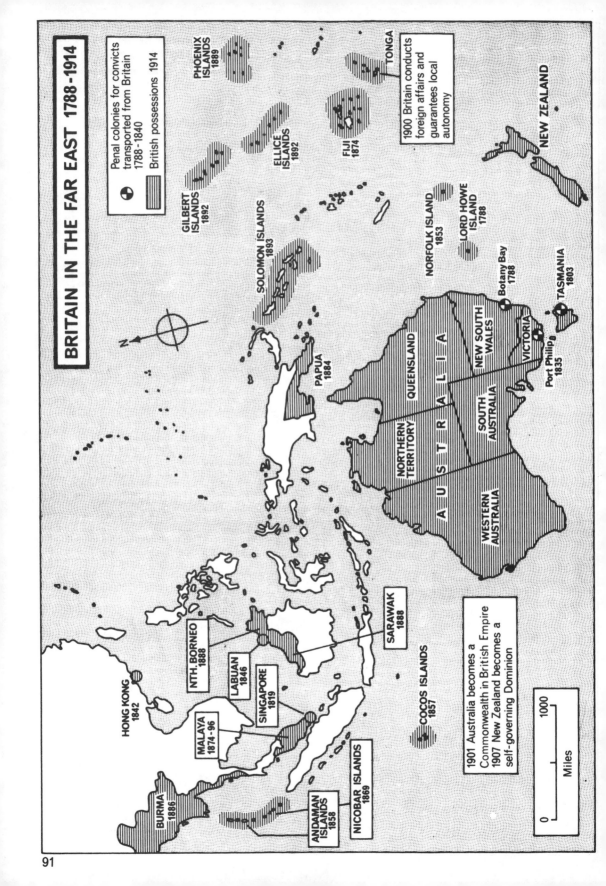

BRITAIN IN THE FAR EAST 1788-1914

Penal colonies for convicts transported from Britain 1788-1840

British possessions 1914

PHOENIX ISLANDS 1889

TONGA

1900 Britain conducts foreign affairs and guarantees local autonomy

NEW ZEALAND

GILBERT ISLANDS 1892

ELLICE ISLANDS 1892

FIJI 1874

SOLOMON ISLANDS 1893

NORFOLK ISLAND 1853

LORD HOWE ISLAND 1788

Botany Bay 1788

TASMANIA 1803

PAPUA 1884

QUEENSLAND

NORTHERN TERRITORY

NEW SOUTH WALES

VICTORIA

Port Philip 1835

A U S T R A L I A

SOUTH AUSTRALIA

WESTERN AUSTRALIA

HONG KONG 1842

NTH. BORNEO 1888

LABUAN 1846

SINGAPORE 1819

SARAWAK 1888

MALAYA 1874-96

COCOS ISLANDS 1857

BURMA 1886

NICOBAR ISLANDS 1869

ANDAMAN ISLANDS 1858

1901 Australia becomes a Commonwealth in British Empire
1907 New Zealand becomes a self-governing Dominion

0   1000

Miles

91

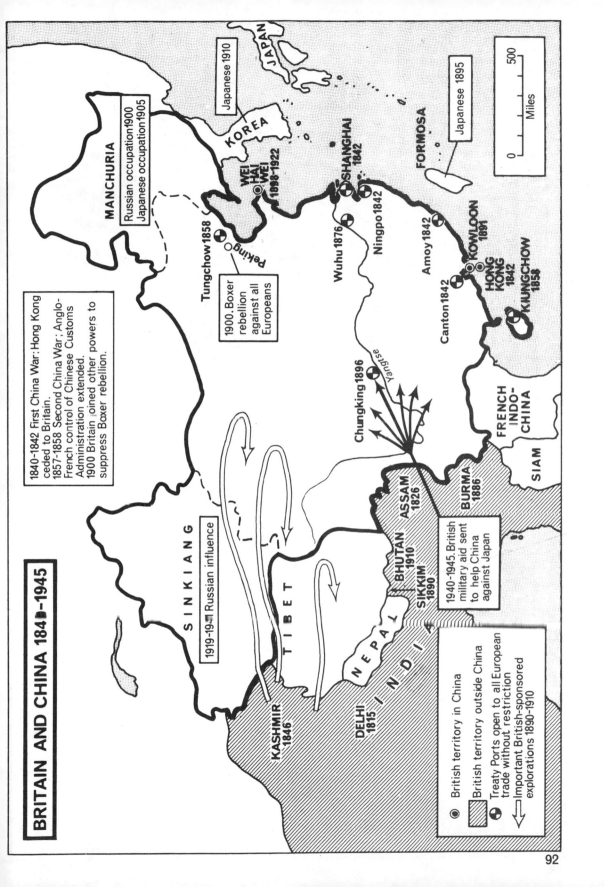

BRITAIN AND CHINA 1840–1945

1840-1842 First China War: Hong Kong ceded to Britain.
1857-1858 Second China War; Anglo-French control of Chinese Customs Administration extended.
1900 Britain joined other powers to suppress Boxer rebellion.

MANCHURIA
Russian occupation 1900
Japanese occupation 1905

Japanese 1910

KOREA

JAPAN

Japanese 1895

FORMOSA

Japanese 1895

500
0   Miles

WEI HAI WEI 1898-1922

SHANGHAI 1842

Tungchow 1858

Peking

1900. Boxer rebellion against all Europeans

Wuhu 1876

Ningpo 1842

Amoy 1842

KOWLOON 1891

Canton 1842

HONG KONG 1842

KUNGCHOW 1858

Chungking 1896

Yangtse

SINKIANG

1919-19.. Russian influence

TIBET

NEPAL

BHUTAN 1910

SIKKIM 1890

ASSAM 1826

BURMA 1886

FRENCH INDO-CHINA

SIAM

1940-1945. British military aid sent to help China against Japan

KASHMIR 1846

DELHI 1815

I N D I A

British territory in China
British territory outside China
Treaty Ports open to all European trade without restriction
Important British-sponsored explorations 1890-1910

92

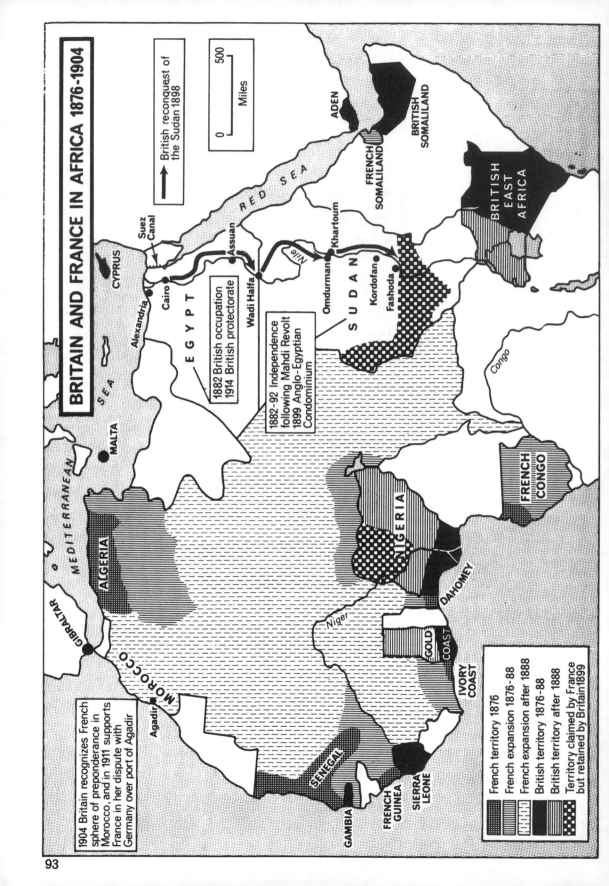

BRITAIN AND FRANCE IN AFRICA 1876-1904

British reconquest of the Sudan 1898

500
0
Miles

1904 Britain recognizes French sphere of preponderance in Morocco, and in 1911 supports France in her dispute with Germany over port of Agadir

1882 British occupation
1914 British protectorate

1882-92 Independence following Mahdi Revolt
1899 Anglo-Egyptian Condominium

MEDITERRANEAN SEA

RED SEA

GIBRALTAR

MALTA

CYPRUS

Alexandria
Cairo
Suez Canal

ALGERIA

MOROCCO

Agadir

E G Y P T

Assuan
Wadi Halfa

Nile

Khartoum
Omdurman
S U D A N
Kordofan
Fashoda

ADEN

FRENCH SOMALILAND

BRITISH SOMALILAND

BRITISH EAST AFRICA

Congo

NIGERIA

DAHOMEY

GOLD COAST

IVORY COAST

SIERRA LEONE

FRENCH GUINEA

GAMBIA

SENEGAL

Niger

FRENCH CONGO

French territory 1876

French expansion 1876-88

French expansion after 1888

British territory 1876-88

British territory after 1888

Territory claimed by France but retained by Britain 1899

93

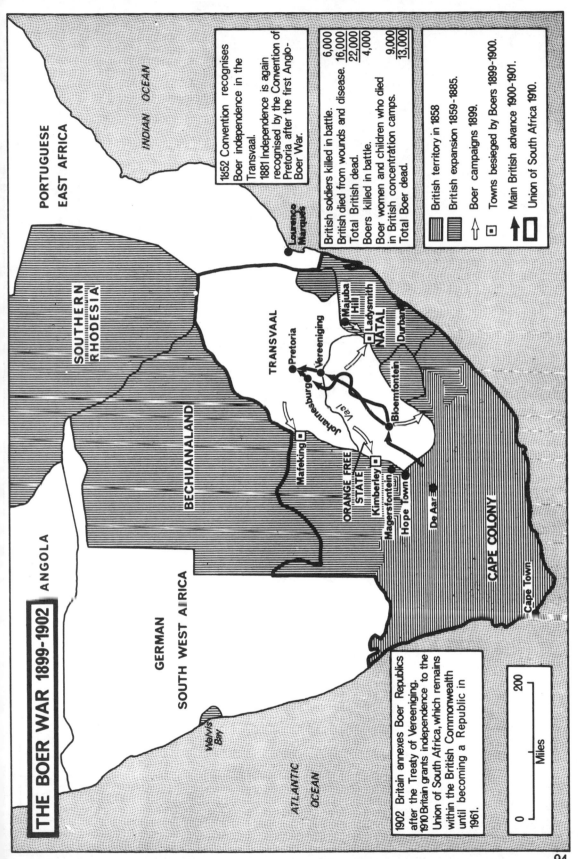

THE BOER WAR 1899-1902

ANGOLA

GERMAN SOUTH WEST AFRICA

PORTUGUESE EAST AFRICA

INDIAN OCEAN

ATLANTIC OCEAN

Malvin's Bay

SOUTHERN RHODESIA

BECHUANALAND

TRANSVAAL

ORANGE FREE STATE

NATAL

CAPE COLONY

Lourenço Marques

Mafeking

Pretoria
Vereeniging
Johannesburg
Vaal
Bloemfontein
Majuba Hill
Ladysmith
Durban
Kimberley
Magersfontein
Hope Town
De Aar
Cape Town

1852 Convention recognises Boer independence in the Transvaal.
1881 Independence is again recognised by the Convention of Pretoria after the first Anglo-Boer War.

British soldiers killed in battle.	6,000
British died from wounds and disease.	16,000
Total British dead.	22,000
Boers killed in battle.	4,000
Boer women and children who died in British concentration camps.	9,000
Total Boer dead.	13,000

British territory in 1858

British expansion 1859 - 1885.

→ Boer campaigns 1899.

☐ Towns besieged by Boers 1899-1900.

Main British advance 1900-1901.

☐ Union of South Africa 1910.

1902 Britain annexes Boer Republics after the Treaty of Vereeniging. 1910 Britain grants independence to the Union of South Africa, which remains within the British Commonwealth until becoming a Republic in 1961.

0   200   Miles

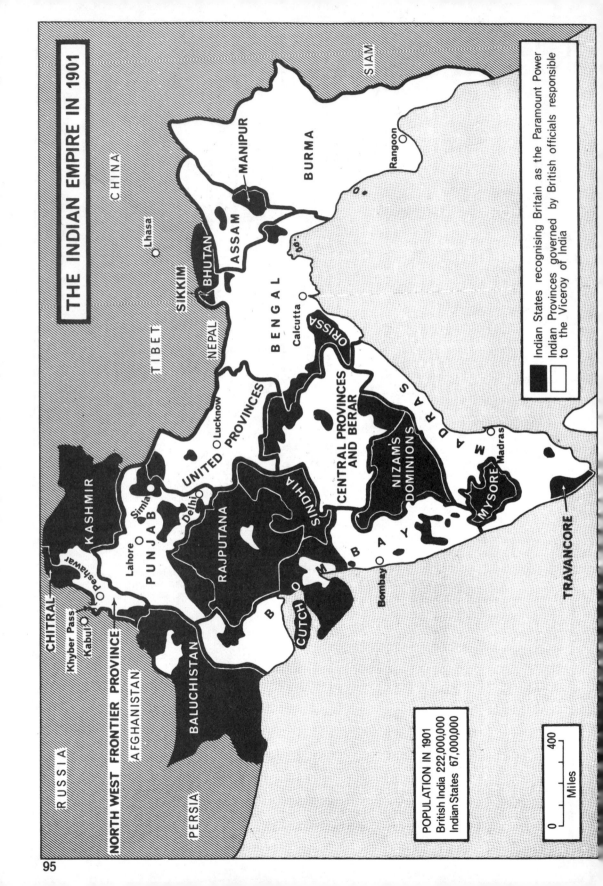

THE INDIAN EMPIRE IN 1901

RUSSIA

CHINA

PERSIA

AFGHANISTAN

TIBET

NEPAL

SIKKIM

BHUTAN

SIAM

○ Lhasa

○ Kabul

Khyber Pass

○ Peshawar

CHITRAL

NORTH WEST FRONTIER PROVINCE

KASHMIR

BALUCHISTAN

PUNJAB

○ Lahore

○ Simla

○ Delhi

UNITED PROVINCES

○ Lucknow

RAJPUTANA

SINDHIA

B

CUTCH

BENGAL

○ Calcutta

ASSAM

MANIPUR

BURMA

ORISSA

○ Rangoon

CENTRAL PROVINCES AND BERAR

NIZAM'S DOMINIONS

MADRAS

MYSORE

○ Madras

TRAVANCORE

B A Y

● Bombay

BOMBAY

POPULATION IN 1901
British India   222,000,000
Indian States   67,000,000

0   400
Miles

◼ Indian States recognising Britain as the Paramount Power

☐ Indian Provinces governed by British officials responsible to the Viceroy of India

95

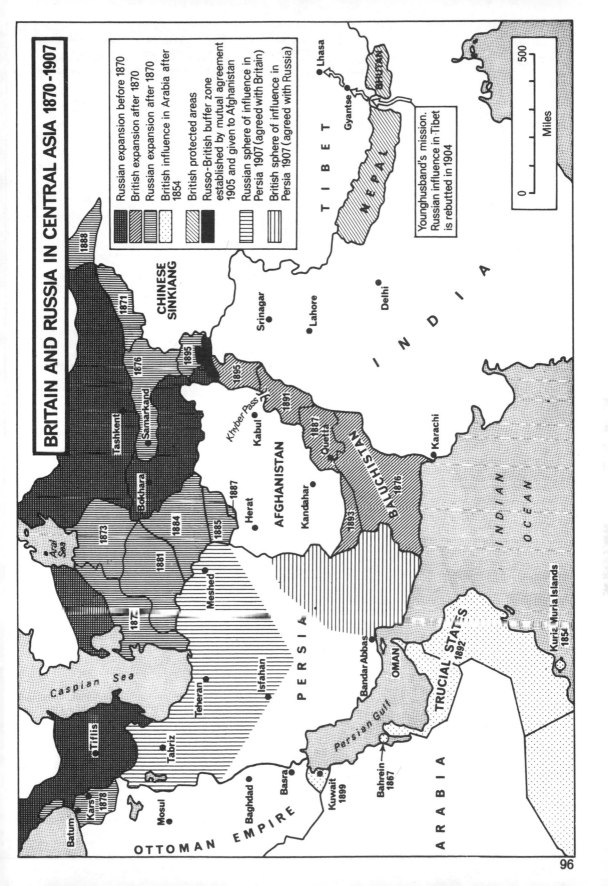

BRITAIN AND RUSSIA IN CENTRAL ASIA 1870-1907

Legend:
- Russian expansion before 1870
- British expansion after 1870
- Russian expansion after 1870
- British influence in Arabia after 1854
- British protected areas
- Russo-British buffer zone established by mutual agreement 1905 and given to Afghanistan
- Russian sphere of influence in Persia 1907 (agreed with Britain)
- British sphere of influence in Persia 1907 (agreed with Russia)

Younghusband's mission. Russian influence in Tibet is rebutted in 1904

Miles 0 — 500

LHASA
Gyantse
TIBET
NEPAL
BHUTAN
INDIA
CHINESE SINKIANG
1888
1871
1876
1895
1895
Srinagar
Lahore
Delhi
Tashkent
Samarkand
Khyber Pass
Kabul
1891
1887
Quetta
Karachi
Bokhara
1887
AFGHANISTAN
BALUCHISTAN
1876
Herat
Kandahar
1893
1873
1884
1885
1881
Meshed
187-
INDIAN OCEAN
PERSIA
Caspian Sea
Isfahan
Teheran
Tabriz
Tiflis
Bandar Abbas
OMAN
TRUCIAL STATES
1892
Kuria Muria Islands
1854
Batum
Kars
1878
Mosul
Baghdad
Basra
Kuwait
1899
Bahrein
1867
Persian Gulf
ARABIA
OTTOMAN EMPIRE

96

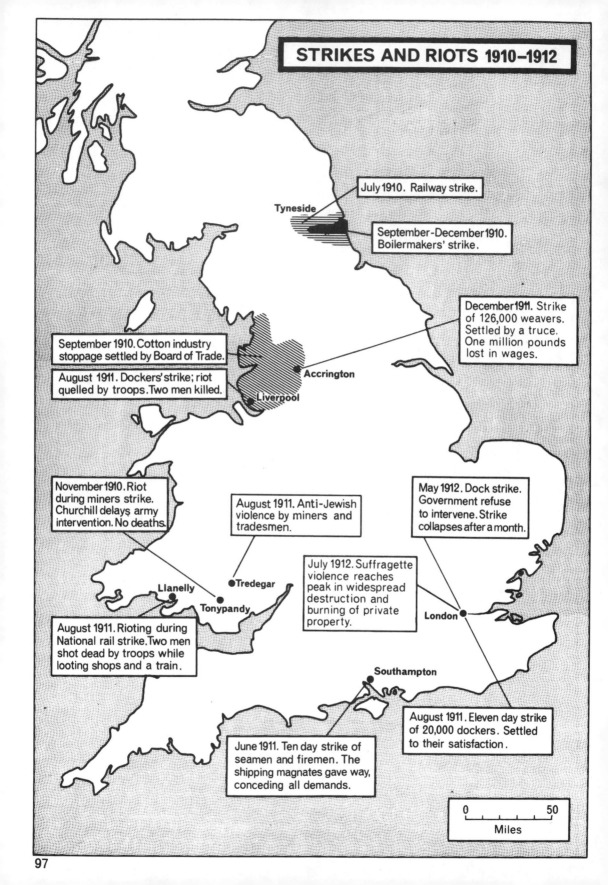

STRIKES AND RIOTS 1910–1912

July 1910. Railway strike.

September–December 1910. Boilermakers' strike.

Tyneside

December 1911. Strike of 126,000 weavers. Settled by a truce. One million pounds lost in wages.

September 1910. Cotton industry stoppage settled by Board of Trade.

August 1911. Dockers' strike; riot quelled by troops. Two men killed.

Accrington

Liverpool

November 1910. Riot during miners strike. Churchill delays army intervention. No deaths.

August 1911. Anti-Jewish violence by miners and tradesmen.

May 1912. Dock strike. Government refuse to intervene. Strike collapses after a month.

July 1912. Suffragette violence reaches peak in widespread destruction and burning of private property.

Llanelly

Tredegar

Tonypandy

London

August 1911. Rioting during National rail strike. Two men shot dead by troops while looting shops and a train.

Southampton

August 1911. Eleven day strike of 20,000 dockers. Settled to their satisfaction.

June 1911. Ten day strike of seamen and firemen. The shipping magnates gave way, conceding all demands.

0   50
Miles

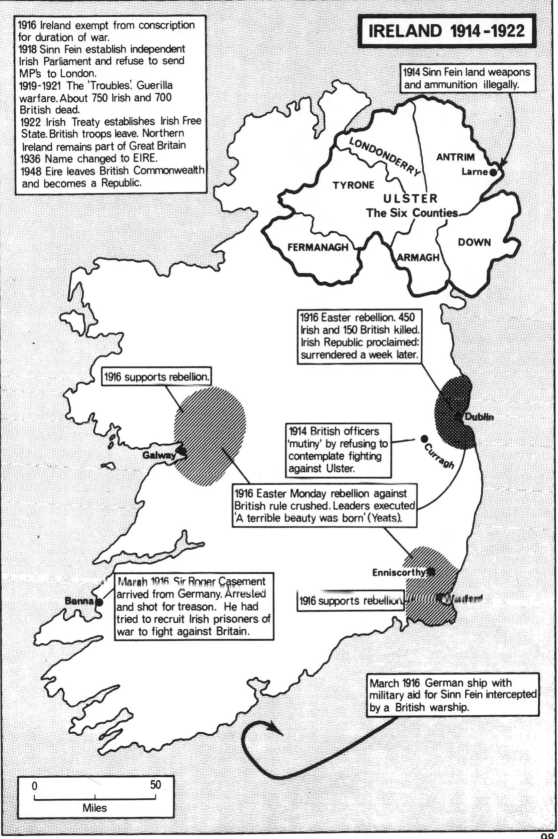

IRELAND 1914-1922

1916 Ireland exempt from conscription for duration of war.
1918 Sinn Fein establish independent Irish Parliament and refuse to send MP's to London.
1919-1921 The 'Troubles'. Guerilla warfare. About 750 Irish and 700 British dead.
1922 Irish Treaty establishes Irish Free State. British troops leave. Northern Ireland remains part of Great Britain
1936 Name changed to EIRE.
1948 Eire leaves British Commonwealth and becomes a Republic.

1914 Sinn Fein land weapons and ammunition illegally.

LONDONDERRY
ANTRIM
Larne
TYRONE
ULSTER
The Six Counties
FERMANAGH
DOWN
ARMAGH

1916 Easter rebellion. 450 Irish and 150 British killed. Irish Republic proclaimed: surrendered a week later.

1916 supports rebellion.

Galway

1914 British officers 'mutiny' by refusing to contemplate fighting against Ulster.

Dublin
Curragh

1916 Easter Monday rebellion against British rule crushed. Leaders executed 'A terrible beauty was born' (Yeats).

March 1916 Sir Roger Casement arrived from Germany. Arrested and shot for treason. He had tried to recruit Irish prisoners of war to fight against Britain.

Banna

Enniscorthy

1916 supports rebellion.
Wexford

March 1916 German ship with military aid for Sinn Fein intercepted by a British warship.

0   50
Miles

98

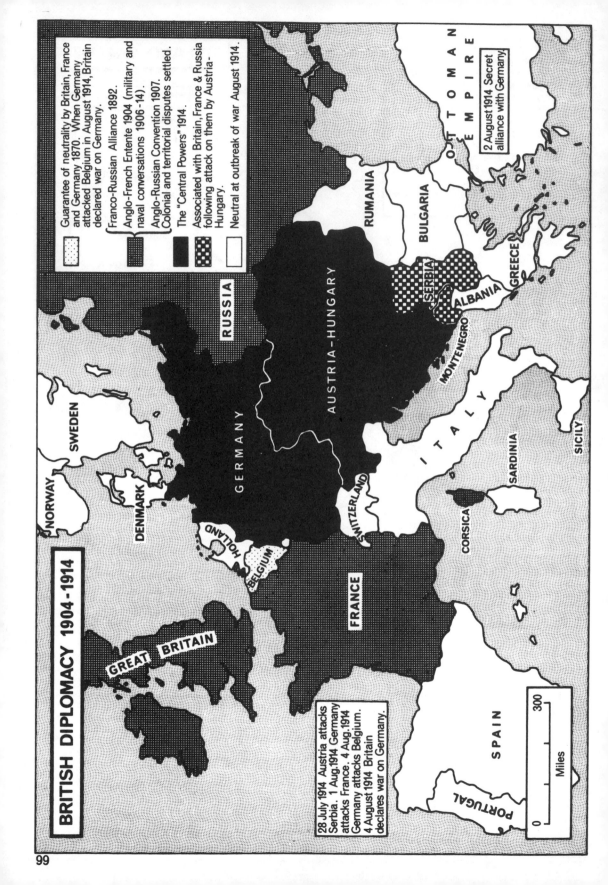

BRITISH DIPLOMACY 1904-1914

Legend:

- Guarantee of neutrality by Britain, France and Germany 1870. When Germany attacked Belgium in August 1914, Britain declared war on Germany.

- Franco-Russian Alliance 1892.

- Anglo-French Entente 1904 (military and naval conversations 1906-14).

- Anglo-Russian Convention 1907. Colonial and territorial disputes settled.

- The "Central Powers" 1914.

- Associated with Britain, France & Russia following attack on them by Austria-Hungary.

- Neutral at outbreak of war August 1914.

2 August 1914 Secret alliance with Germany.

28 July 1914 Austria attacks Serbia. 1 Aug.1914 Germany attacks France. 4 Aug.1914 Germany attacks Belgium. 4 August 1914 Britain declares war on Germany.

NORWAY

SWEDEN

DENMARK

GREAT BRITAIN

HOLLAND

BELGIUM

GERMANY

FRANCE

SWITZERLAND

SPAIN

PORTUGAL

CORSICA

SARDINIA

ITALY

SICILY

RUSSIA

AUSTRIA-HUNGARY

RUMANIA

SERBIA

MONTENEGRO

ALBANIA

BULGARIA

GREECE

OTTOMAN EMPIRE

Miles

0   300

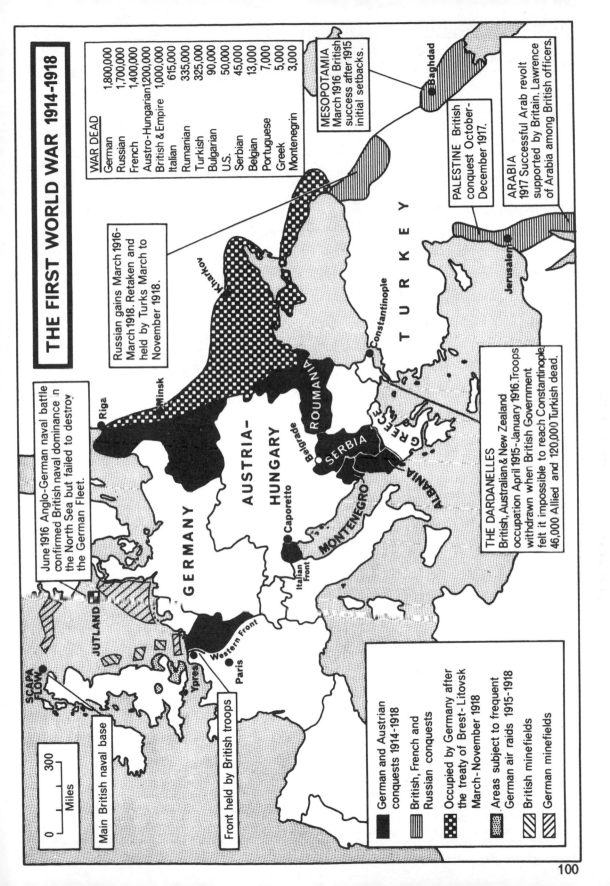

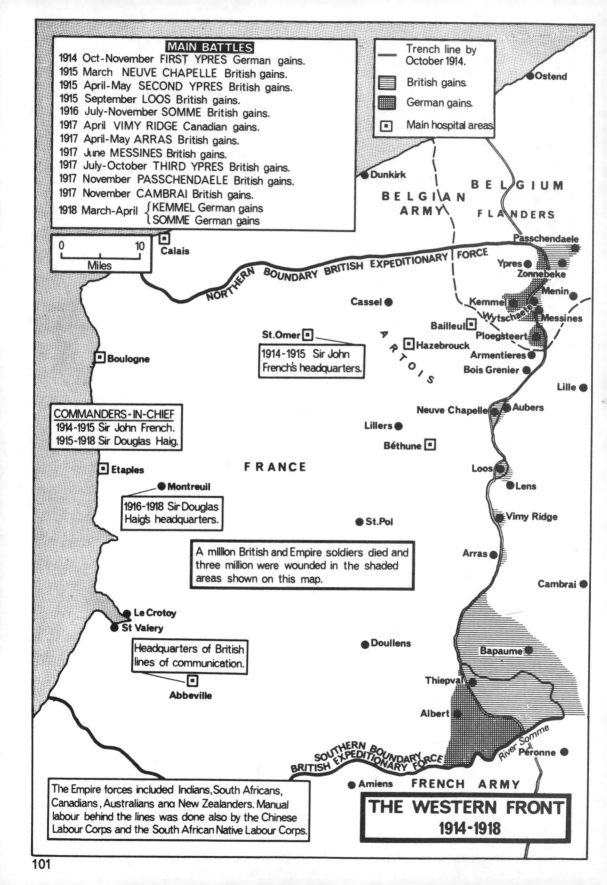

MAIN BATTLES

1914 Oct-November FIRST YPRES German gains.
1915 March NEUVE CHAPELLE British gains.
1915 April-May SECOND YPRES British gains.
1915 September LOOS British gains.
1916 July-November SOMME British gains.
1917 April VIMY RIDGE Canadian gains.
1917 April-May ARRAS British gains.
1917 June MESSINES British gains.
1917 July-October THIRD YPRES British gains.
1917 November PASSCHENDAELE British gains.
1917 November CAMBRAI British gains.
1918 March-April { KEMMEL German gains
                   { SOMME German gains

Trench line by
October 1914.

British gains.

German gains.

Main hospital areas.

0   10
Miles

NORTHERN BOUNDARY BRITISH EXPEDITIONARY FORCE

BELGIAN
ARMY

BELGIUM
FLANDERS

Ostend

Dunkirk

Calais

Passchendaele
Ypres
Zonnebeke
Menin
Kemmel
Wytschaete
Messines
Ploegsteert
Armentieres
Bois Grenier
Lille

Cassel

St.Omer

1914-1915 Sir John
French's headquarters.

Bailleul
Hazebrouck

ARTOIS

Boulogne

Neuve Chapelle
Aubers

COMMANDERS-IN-CHIEF
1914-1915 Sir John French.
1915-1918 Sir Douglas Haig.

Lillers

Béthune

FRANCE

Loos
Lens

Etaples

Montreuil

1916-1918 Sir Douglas
Haig's headquarters.

St.Pol

Vimy Ridge

A million British and Empire soldiers died and
three million were wounded in the shaded
areas shown on this map.

Arras

Cambrai

Le Crotoy
St Valery

Headquarters of British
lines of communication.

Abbeville

Doullens

Bapaume

Thiepval

Albert

SOUTHERN BOUNDARY
BRITISH EXPEDITIONARY FORCE

River Somme
Péronne

The Empire forces included Indians, South Africans,
Canadians, Australians and New Zealanders. Manual
labour behind the lines was done also by the Chinese
Labour Corps and the South African Native Labour Corps.

Amiens

FRENCH ARMY

THE WESTERN FRONT
1914-1918

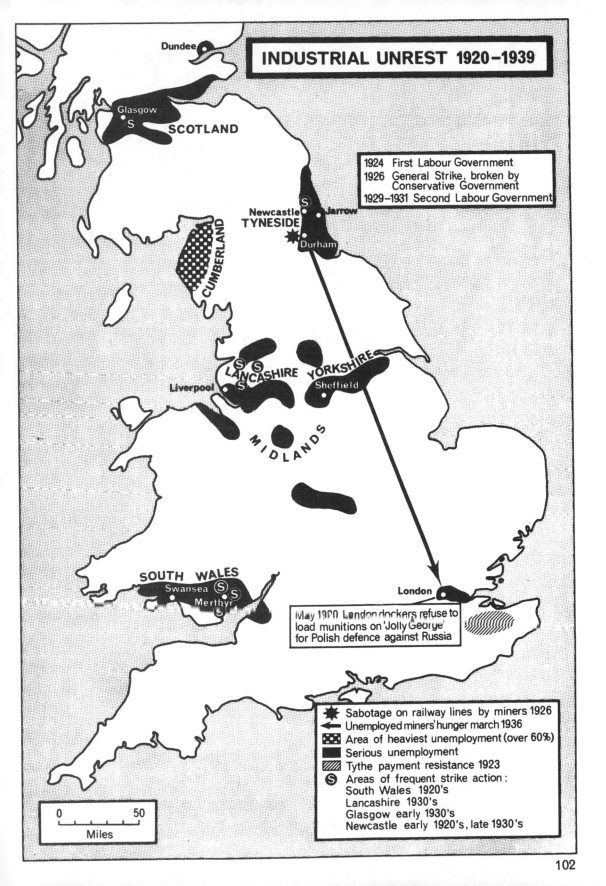

INDUSTRIAL UNREST 1920–1939

Dundee

Glasgow
S

SCOTLAND

1924 First Labour Government
1926 General Strike, broken by
Conservative Government
1929–1931 Second Labour Government

CUMBERLAND

Newcastle S
TYNESIDE Jarrow
Durham

LANCASHIRE S S YORKSHIRE
S
Liverpool Sheffield

MIDLANDS

SOUTH WALES
Swansea S S
Merthyr

London

May 1920 London dockers refuse to
load munitions on 'Jolly George'
for Polish defence against Russia

★ Sabotage on railway lines by miners 1926
← Unemployed miners' hunger march 1936
▨ Area of heaviest unemployment (over 60%)
■ Serious unemployment
▨ Tythe payment resistance 1923
S Areas of frequent strike action:
South Wales 1920's
Lancashire 1930's
Glasgow early 1930's
Newcastle early 1920's, late 1930's

0 ___ 50
Miles

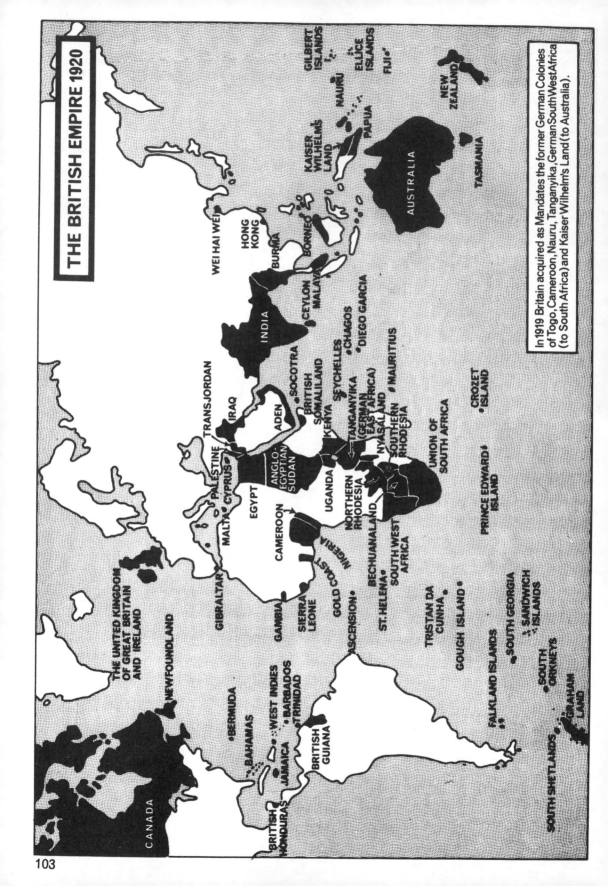

THE BRITISH EMPIRE 1920

In 1919 Britain acquired as Mandates the former German Colonies of Togo, Cameroon, Nauru, Tanganyika, German South West Africa (to South Africa) and Kaiser Wilhelm's Land (to Australia).

CANADA

NEWFOUNDLAND

THE UNITED KINGDOM OF GREAT BRITAIN AND IRELAND

BERMUDA

BAHAMAS

WEST INDIES
JAMAICA
BARBADOS
TRINIDAD

BRITISH HONDURAS

BRITISH GUIANA

GIBRALTAR

GAMBIA

SERRA LEONE

GOLD COAST

NIGERIA

ASCENSION

ST. HELENA

TRISTAN DA CUNHA

GOUGH ISLAND

FALKLAND ISLANDS

SOUTH GEORGIA

SANDWICH ISLANDS

SOUTH ORKNEYS

SOUTH SHETLANDS

GRAHAM LAND

PALESTINE
MALTA
CYPRUS
EGYPT
TRANS-JORDAN
IRAQ
ADEN
ANGLO-EGYPTIAN SUDAN
SOCOTRA
BRITISH SOMALILAND
SEYCHELLES
CHAGOS
DIEGO GARCIA
UGANDA
KENYA
TANGANYIKA (GERMAN EAST AFRICA)
NYASALAND
NORTHERN RHODESIA
SOUTHERN RHODESIA
MAURITIUS
CAMEROON
BECHUANALAND
SOUTH WEST AFRICA
UNION OF SOUTH AFRICA
PRINCE EDWARD ISLAND
CROZET ISLAND

WEI HAI WEI

HONG KONG

BURMA

INDIA

CEYLON
MALAYA

BORNEO

NEW ZEALAND

TASMANIA

AUSTRALIA

PAPUA

KAISER WILHELM'S LAND

NAURU

GILBERT ISLANDS

ELLICE ISLANDS

FIJI

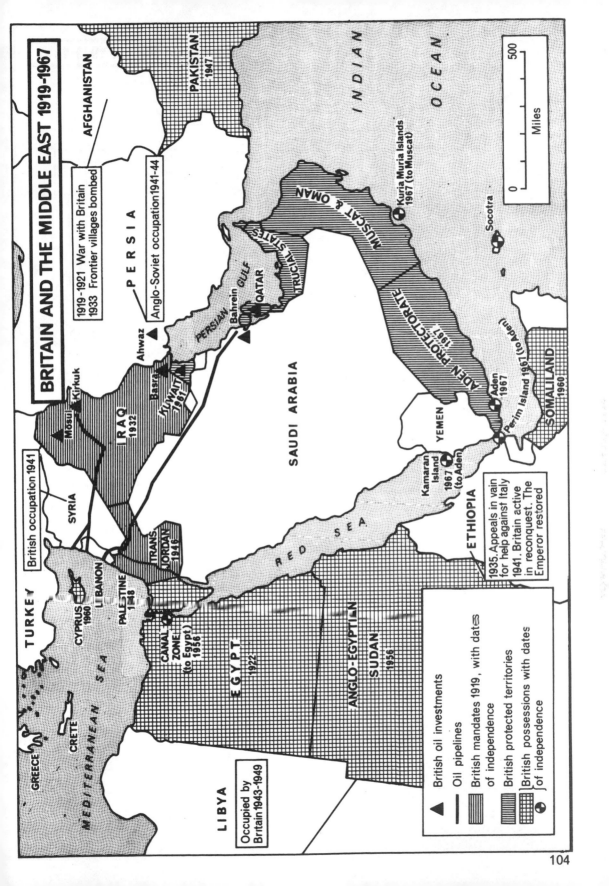

BRITAIN AND THE MIDDLE EAST 1919-1967

AFGHANISTAN

PAKISTAN
1947

PERSIA

1919-1921 War with Britain
1933 Frontier villages bombed

Anglo-Soviet occupation 1941-44

INDIAN

OCEAN

Ahwaz

PERSIAN GULF

Bahrein
QATAR

MUSCAT & OMAN

TRUCIAL STATES

Kuria Muria Islands
1967 (to Muscat)

Socotra

Kirkuk
Mosul

Basra

KUWAIT
1961

SAUDI ARABIA

ADEN PROTECTORATE

Aden 1967

Perim Island 1967 (to Aden)

SOMALILAND
1960

IRAQ
1932

SYRIA

British occupation 1941

YEMEN

Kamaran
Island
1967
(to Aden)

ETHIOPIA

1935. Appeals in vain
for help against Italy
1941. Britain active
in reconquest. The
Emperor restored

TRANS-
JORDAN
1946

LEBANON

PALESTINE
1948

RED SEA

TURKEY

CYPRUS
1960

British occupation 1941

CRETE

GREECE

MEDITERRANEAN SEA

CANAL
ZONE
(to Egypt)
1956

EGYPT
1922

ANGLO-EGYPTIAN
SUDAN
1956

LIBYA

Occupied by Britain 1943-1949

▲ British oil investments

— Oil pipelines

British mandates 1919, with dates
of independence

British protected territories

British possessions with dates
of independence

0   500
Miles

104

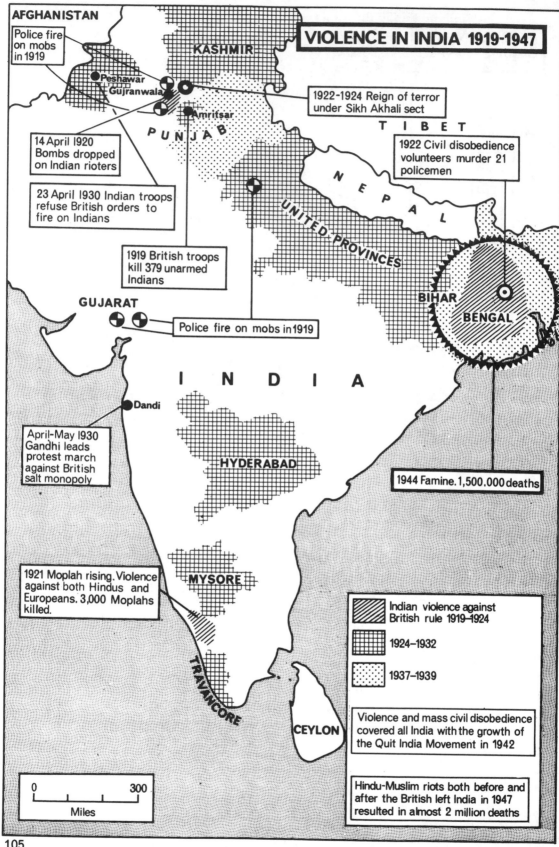

VIOLENCE IN INDIA 1919-1947

AFGHANISTAN

Police fire on mobs in 1919

KASHMIR

Peshawar
Gujranwala
Amritsar

1922-1924 Reign of terror under Sikh Akhali sect

PUNJAB

T I B E T

14 April 1920 Bombs dropped on Indian rioters

1922 Civil disobedience volunteers murder 21 policemen

23 April 1930 Indian troops refuse British orders to fire on Indians

N E P A L

UNITED PROVINCES

1919 British troops kill 379 unarmed Indians

BIHAR
BENGAL

GUJARAT

Police fire on mobs in 1919

I N D I A

Dandi

April-May 1930 Gandhi leads protest march against British salt monopoly

1944 Famine. 1,500,000 deaths

HYDERABAD

1921 Moplah rising. Violence against both Hindus and Europeans. 3,000 Moplahs killed.

MYSORE

TRAVANCORE

CEYLON

Indian violence against British rule 1919–1924

1924–1932

1937–1939

Violence and mass civil disobedience covered all India with the growth of the Quit India Movement in 1942

Hindu-Muslim riots both before and after the British left India in 1947 resulted in almost 2 million deaths

0   300
Miles

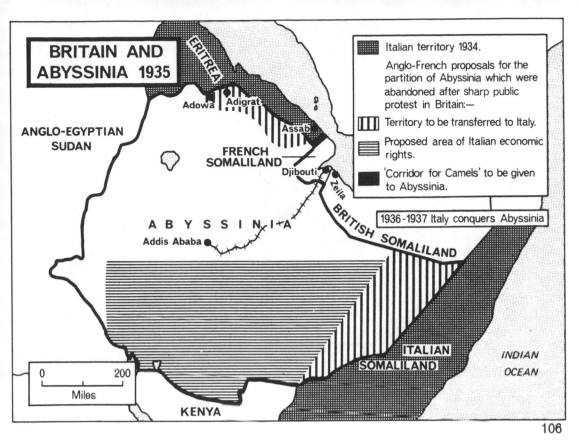

BRITAIN AND ABYSSINIA 1935

ERITREA

Adowa Adigrat

Assab

ANGLO-EGYPTIAN SUDAN

FRENCH SOMALILAND

Djibouti

Zeila

BRITISH SOMALILAND

A B Y S S I N I A

Addis Ababa

ITALIAN SOMALILAND

INDIAN OCEAN

0   200
Miles

KENYA

Italian territory 1934.

Anglo-French proposals for the partition of Abyssinia which were abandoned after sharp public protest in Britain:—

Territory to be transferred to Italy.

Proposed area of Italian economic rights.

'Corridor for Camels' to be given to Abyssinia.

1936-1937 Italy conquers Abyssinia

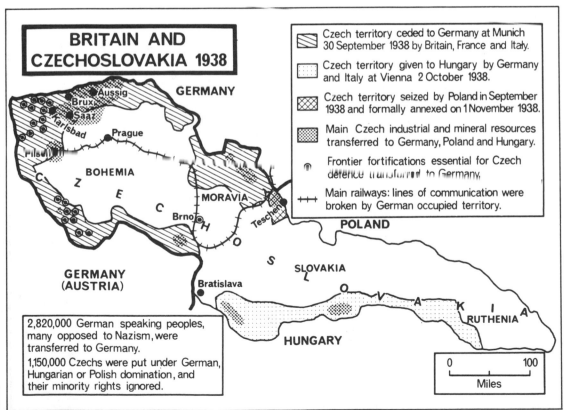

BRITAIN AND CZECHOSLOVAKIA 1938

GERMANY

Aussig
Brux
Saaz
Karlsbad
Prague
Pilsen

BOHEMIA

C
Z
E
C
H
O
S
L
O
V
A
K
I
A

MORAVIA

Brno

Teschen

POLAND

GERMANY (AUSTRIA)

Bratislava

SLOVAKIA

RUTHENIA

HUNGARY

Czech territory ceded to Germany at Munich 30 September 1938 by Britain, France and Italy.

Czech territory given to Hungary by Germany and Italy at Vienna 2 October 1938.

Czech territory seized by Poland in September 1938 and formally annexed on 1 November 1938.

Main Czech industrial and mineral resources transferred to Germany, Poland and Hungary.

Frontier fortifications essential for Czech defence transferred to Germany.

Main railways: lines of communication were broken by German occupied territory.

0   100
Miles

2,820,000 German speaking peoples, many opposed to Nazism, were transferred to Germany.

1,150,000 Czechs were put under German, Hungarian or Polish domination, and their minority rights ignored.

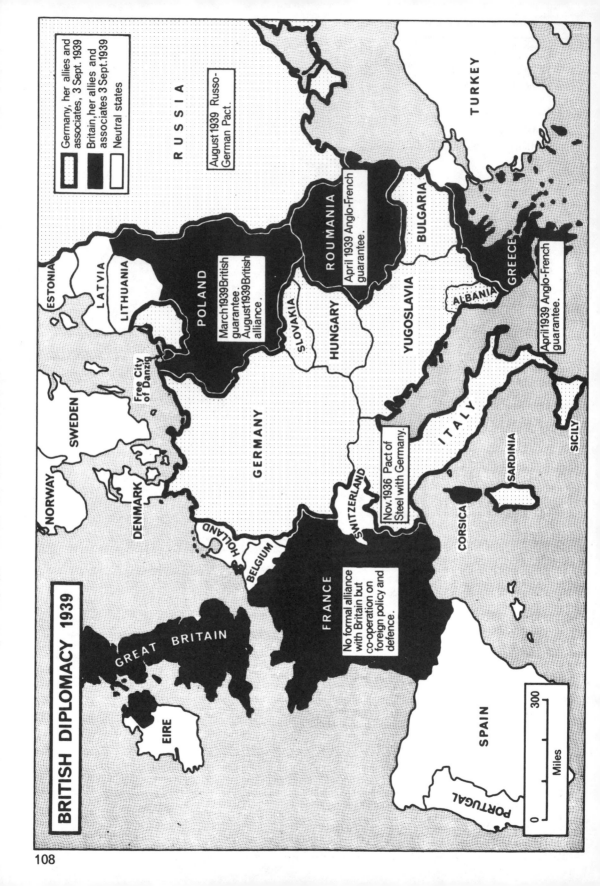

BRITISH DIPLOMACY 1939

Germany, her allies and associates, 3 Sept. 1939

Britain, her allies and associates 3 Sept.1939

Neutral states

August 1939 Russo-German Pact.

R U S S I A

TURKEY

ESTONIA

LATVIA

LITHUANIA

POLAND

March1939British guarantee. August1939British alliance.

ROUMANIA

April 1939 Anglo-French guarantee.

BULGARIA

GREECE

April1939 Anglo-French guarantee.

Free City of Danzig

SLOVAKIA

HUNGARY

YUGOSLAVIA

ALBANIA

SWEDEN

GERMANY

Nov. 1936 Pact of Steel with Germany.

ITALY

SARDINIA

SICILY

NORWAY

DENMARK

HOLLAND

BELGIUM

SWITZERLAND

FRANCE

No formal alliance with Britain but co-operation on foreign policy and defence.

CORSICA

GREAT BRITAIN

EIRE

SPAIN

PORTUGAL

0 — 300 Miles

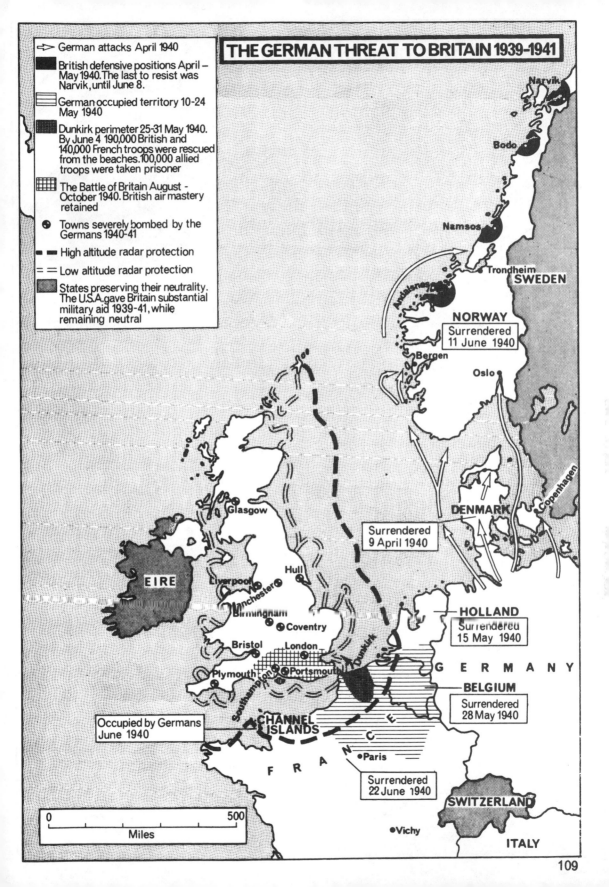

THE GERMAN THREAT TO BRITAIN 1939-1941

Legend:

- ⇨ German attacks April 1940
- ■ British defensive positions April – May 1940. The last to resist was Narvik, until June 8.
- ▤ German occupied territory 10-24 May 1940
- ■ Dunkirk perimeter 25-31 May 1940. By June 4 190,000 British and 140,000 French troops were rescued from the beaches. 100,000 allied troops were taken prisoner
- ▦ The Battle of Britain August - October 1940. British air mastery retained
- ⊕ Towns severely bombed by the Germans 1940-41
- ▬ ▬ High altitude radar protection
- ═ ═ Low altitude radar protection
- ▨ States preserving their neutrality. The U.S.A. gave Britain substantial military aid 1939-41, while remaining neutral

Narvik

Bodo

Namsos

Trondheim

SWEDEN

NORWAY
Surrendered 11 June 1940

Bergen

Oslo

DENMARK
Surrendered 9 April 1940

Copenhagen

Glasgow

EIRE

Hull

Liverpool

Manchester

Birmingham

⊙ Coventry

Bristol

London

Plymouth

Southampton ⊙ Portsmouth

Dunkirk

HOLLAND
Surrendered 15 May 1940

G E R M A N Y

BELGIUM
Surrendered 28 May 1940

CHANNEL ISLANDS
Occupied by Germans June 1940

F R A N C E

• Paris

Surrendered 22 June 1940

SWITZERLAND

• Vichy

ITALY

0		500
	Miles	

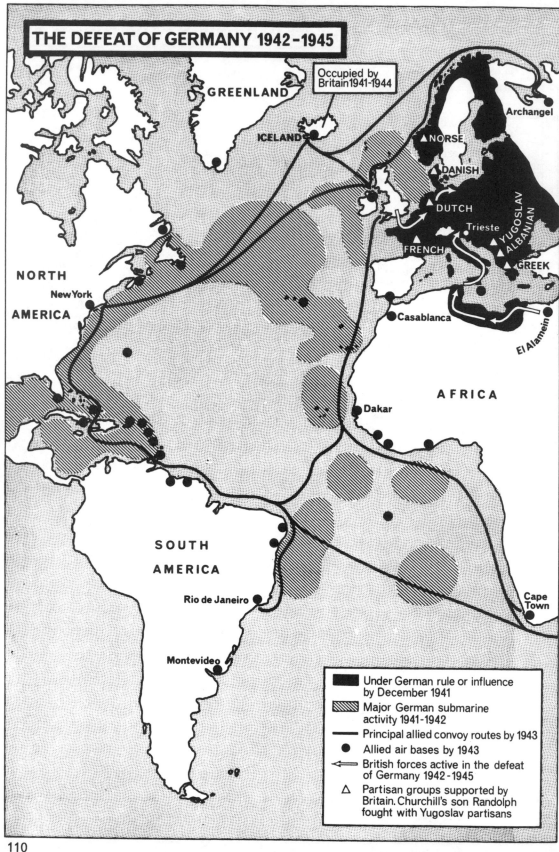

THE DEFEAT OF GERMANY 1942-1945

GREENLAND

Occupied by
Britain 1941-1944

ICELAND

Archangel

NORSE

DANISH

DUTCH

Trieste

YUGOSLAV

NORTH

ALBANIAN

AMERICA

FRENCH

GREEK

New York

Casablanca

El Alamein

AFRICA

Dakar

SOUTH

AMERICA

Rio de Janeiro

Cape
Town

Montevideo

■ Under German rule or influence
by December 1941

▨ Major German submarine
activity 1941-1942

━ Principal allied convoy routes by 1943

● Allied air bases by 1943

← British forces active in the defeat
of Germany 1942-1945

△ Partisan groups supported by
Britain. Churchill's son Randolph
fought with Yugoslav partisans

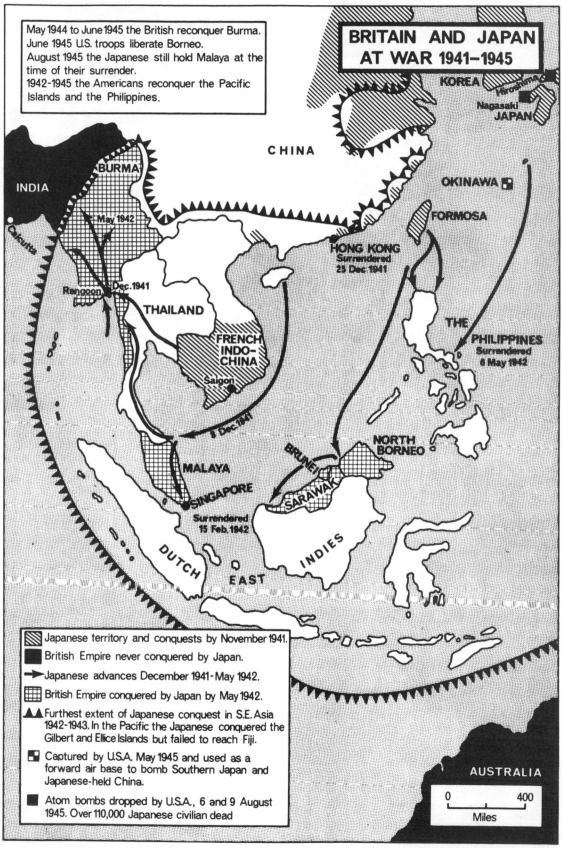

May 1944 to June 1945 the British reconquer Burma.
June 1945 U.S. troops liberate Borneo.
August 1945 the Japanese still hold Malaya at the time of their surrender.
1942-1945 the Americans reconquer the Pacific Islands and the Philippines.

BRITAIN AND JAPAN AT WAR 1941–1945

KOREA

Hiroshima

Nagasaki

JAPAN

CHINA

OKINAWA

FORMOSA

BURMA

INDIA

Calcutta

May 1942

HONG KONG
Surrendered
25 Dec 1941

Rangoon

8 Dec.1941

THAILAND

THE PHILIPPINES
Surrendered
6 May 1942

FRENCH INDO-CHINA

Saigon

8 Dec.1941

NORTH BORNEO

BRUNEI

MALAYA

SINGAPORE
Surrendered
15 Feb. 1942

SARAWAK

DUTCH

EAST

INDIES

Japanese territory and conquests by November 1941.

British Empire never conquered by Japan.

Japanese advances December 1941-May 1942.

British Empire conquered by Japan by May 1942.

Furthest extent of Japanese conquest in S.E. Asia 1942-1943. In the Pacific the Japanese conquered the Gilbert and Ellice Islands but failed to reach Fiji.

Captured by U.S.A. May 1945 and used as a forward air base to bomb Southern Japan and Japanese-held China.

Atom bombs dropped by U.S.A., 6 and 9 August 1945. Over 110,000 Japanese civilian dead

AUSTRALIA

0   400
Miles

111

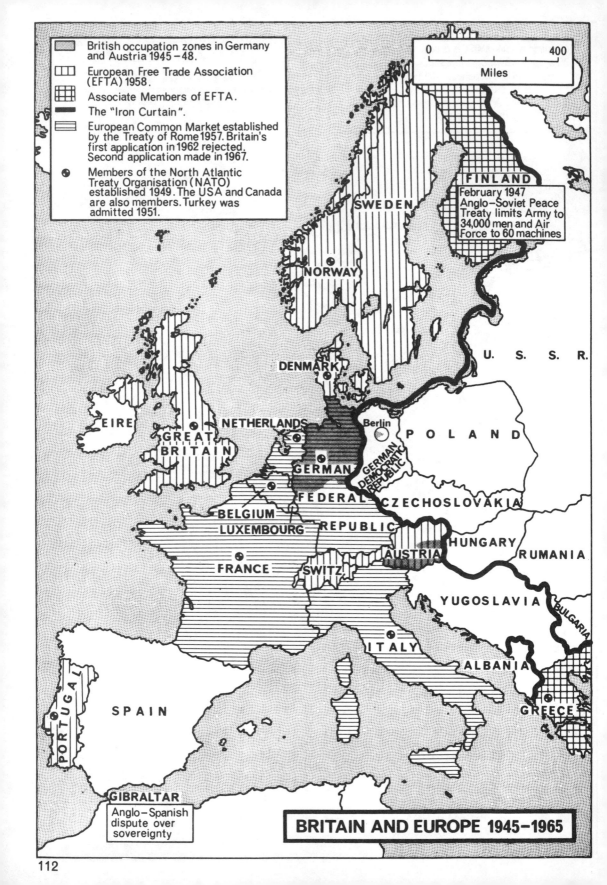

Britain and Europe 1945–1965

Legend:
- British occupation zones in Germany and Austria 1945–48.
- European Free Trade Association (EFTA) 1958.
- Associate Members of EFTA.
- The "Iron Curtain".
- European Common Market established by the Treaty of Rome 1957. Britain's first application in 1962 rejected. Second application made in 1967.
- ⊕ Members of the North Atlantic Treaty Organisation (NATO) established 1949. The USA and Canada are also members. Turkey was admitted 1951.

0 — 400 Miles

FINLAND
February 1947 Anglo–Soviet Peace Treaty limits Army to 34,000 men and Air Force to 60 machines

SWEDEN

NORWAY

DENMARK

EIRE

GREAT BRITAIN

NETHERLANDS

BELGIUM

LUXEMBOURG

FRANCE

SWITZ

GERMAN FEDERAL REPUBLIC

Berlin

GERMAN DEMOCRATIC REPUBLIC

POLAND

U. S. S. R.

CZECHOSLOVAKIA

AUSTRIA

HUNGARY

RUMANIA

YUGOSLAVIA

BULGARIA

ITALY

ALBANIA

GREECE

SPAIN

PORTUGAL

GIBRALTAR
Anglo–Spanish dispute over sovereignty

BRITAIN AND EUROPE 1945–1965

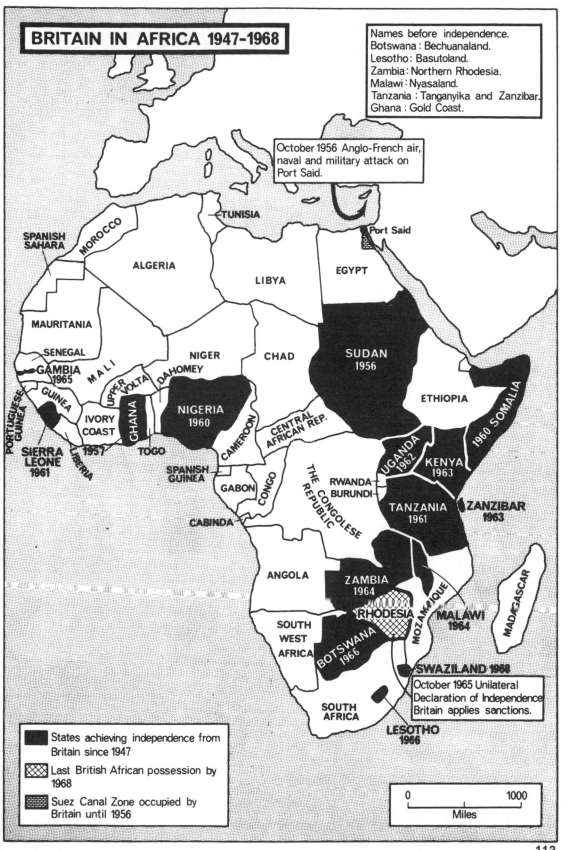

BRITAIN IN AFRICA 1947-1968

Names before independence.
Botswana : Bechuanaland.
Lesotho : Basutoland.
Zambia : Northern Rhodesia.
Malawi : Nyasaland.
Tanzania : Tanganyika and Zanzibar.
Ghana : Gold Coast.

October 1956 Anglo-French air, naval and military attack on Port Said.

Port Said

SPANISH SAHARA
MOROCCO
TUNISIA
ALGERIA
LIBYA
EGYPT
MAURITANIA
SENEGAL
GAMBIA 1965
MALI
NIGER
CHAD
SUDAN 1956
ETHIOPIA
GUINEA
UPPER VOLTA
DAHOMEY
PORTUGUESE GUINEA
SIERRA LEONE 1961
LIBERIA
IVORY COAST
GHANA 1957
TOGO
NIGERIA 1960
CAMEROON
SPANISH GUINEA
CENTRAL AFRICAN REP.
1960 SOMALIA
UGANDA 1962
KENYA 1963
GABON
CONGO
THE CONGOLESE REPUBLIC
RWANDA
BURUNDI
TANZANIA 1961
ZANZIBAR 1963
CABINDA
ANGOLA
ZAMBIA 1964
MOZAMBIQUE
MADAGASCAR
SOUTH WEST AFRICA
RHODESIA
MALAWI 1964
BOTSWANA 1966
SWAZILAND 1968
SOUTH AFRICA
LESOTHO 1966

October 1965 Unilateral Declaration of Independence Britain applies sanctions.

States achieving independence from Britain since 1947

Last British African possession by 1968

Suez Canal Zone occupied by Britain until 1956

0   1000
Miles

UNIVERSITY FOUNDATIONS 1264–1967

0 — 50
Miles

Aberdeen 1495

Dundee 1967

St. Andrews 1410

1967 Stirling

Glasgow 1451
Strathclyde 1964

Edinburgh 1583

Heriot-Watt 1966

Newcastle 1963

Durham 1832

Lancaster 1964

York 1963

Leeds 1904

Hull 1954

Bradford 1966

Liverpool 1903

Manchester 1851

Salford 1967

Sheffield 1905

Bangor

Keele 1962

Nottingham 1938

1966 Loughborough

Leicester 1957

East Anglia 1964

University of Wales 1893

Aberystwyth

Aston 1966
Birmingham 1900

Warwick 1965

Cambridge 1284

Essex 1965

Swansea

Cardiff

Oxford 1264

Brunel 1966

Reading 1926

Surrey 1966

London 1836

The City University 1966

Kent 1965

Bristol 1909

Bath 1966

Southampton 1952

Sussex 1961

Exeter 1955

● Founded 1264–1583
● Nineteenth century foundations
◑ Founded 1900–1938
◕ Founded 1952–1967

114

BRITAIN 1945-1966

Continuous growth of population 1930-1960
Continuous fall of population 1930-1960
● Towns where more than 10% of the population in private dwellings live two to a room (figures for 1958)
● New towns built since 1945
◎ Oil Refineries 1966
⊕ Nuclear Power Stations in operation by 1966
○ Drillings for Natural Gas 1964-1966
⊙ Hydro-electric power stations

MAIN WAVES OF IMMIGRANTS
1880-1905 RUSSIAN JEWISH REFUGEES
1933-1939 GERMAN JEWISH REFUGEES
1956 HUNGARIAN REFUGEES
1956-1960 INDIAN, PAKISTANI AND WEST INDIAN IMMIGRANTS

POPULATION IN 1961: 50,368,455
of whom nearly 8 million in London area

Dounreay
Cumbernauld
Glenrothes
Livingston
East Kilbride
Hunterston
Chapel Cross
Washington
Peterlee
Newton Aycliffe
Calder Hall
North Sea
Springfields
Skelmersdale
Wylfa
Runcorn
Capenhurst
Trawsfynydd
Dawley
Corby
Sizewell
Stevenage
Hemel Hempstead
Welwyn
Harlow
Bradwell
Hatfield
Basildon
Milford Haven
Cwmbran
Berkeley
Oldbury
Bracknell
Crawley
Dungeness
Hinkley Point
Fawley

0   60
Miles

1945-1965 ROAD DEAD 121,797

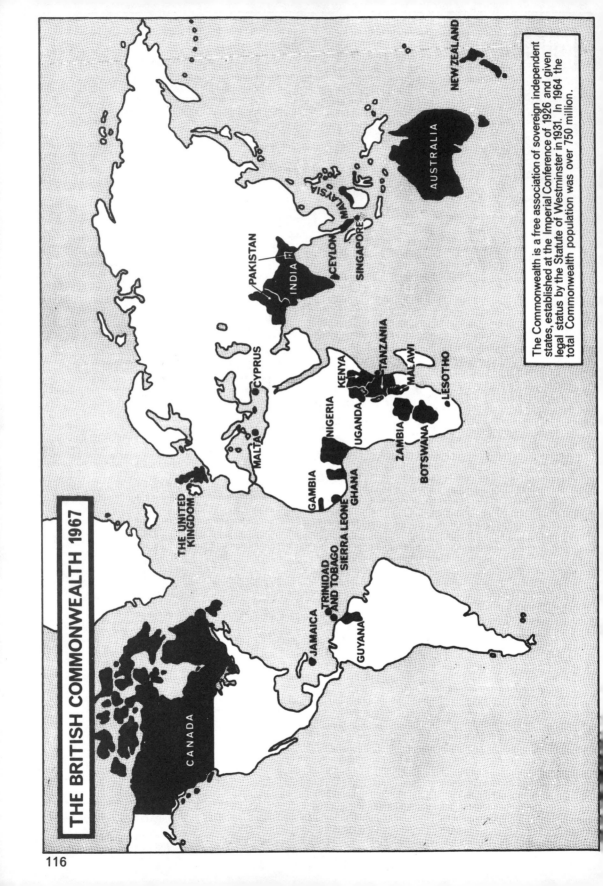

THE BRITISH COMMONWEALTH 1967

The Commonwealth is a free association of sovereign independent states, established at the Imperial Conference of 1926 and given legal status by the Statute of Westminster in 1931. In 1964 the total Commonwealth population was over 750 million.

CANADA

THE UNITED KINGDOM

JAMAICA

TRINIDAD AND TOBAGO

SIERRA LEONE

GUYANA

GAMBIA

GHANA

NIGERIA

UGANDA

MALTA

CYPRUS

PAKISTAN

INDIA

CEYLON

MALAYSIA

SINGAPORE

KENYA

TANZANIA

MALAWI

LESOTHO

ZAMBIA

BOTSWANA

AUSTRALIA

NEW ZEALAND

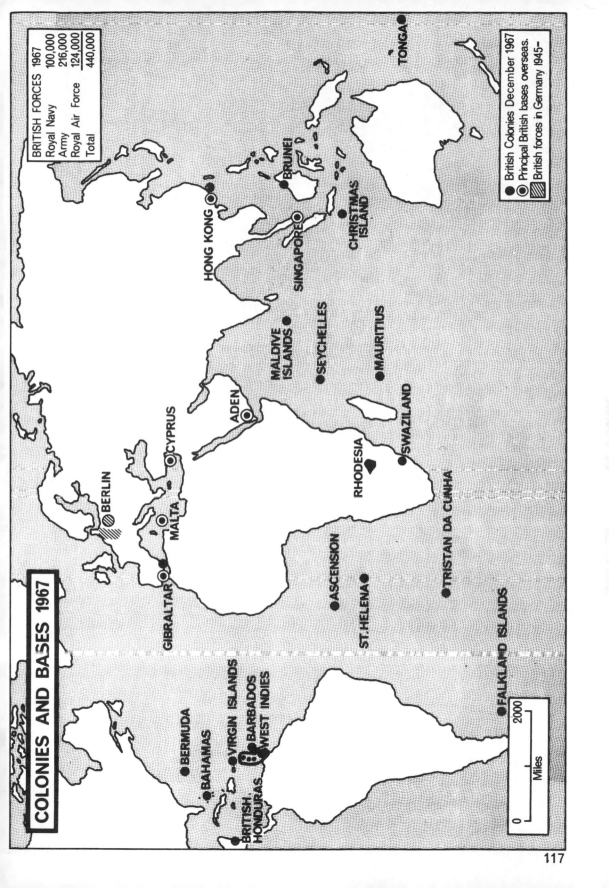

COLONIES AND BASES 1967

BRITISH FORCES 1967	
Royal Navy	100,000
Army	216,000
Royal Air Force	124,000
Total	440,000

● British Colonies December 1967
◎ Principal British bases overseas.
▨ British forces in Germany 1945–

TONGA

HONG KONG

BRUNEI

SINGAPORE

CHRISTMAS ISLAND

MALDIVE ISLANDS

SEYCHELLES

MAURITIUS

ADEN

CYPRUS

SWAZILAND

RHODESIA

BERLIN

MALTA

GIBRALTAR

ASCENSION

ST. HELENA

TRISTAN DA CUNHA

FALKLAND ISLANDS

BERMUDA

BAHAMAS

VIRGIN ISLANDS

BARBADOS WEST INDIES

BRITISH HONDURAS

0   2000
Miles

117

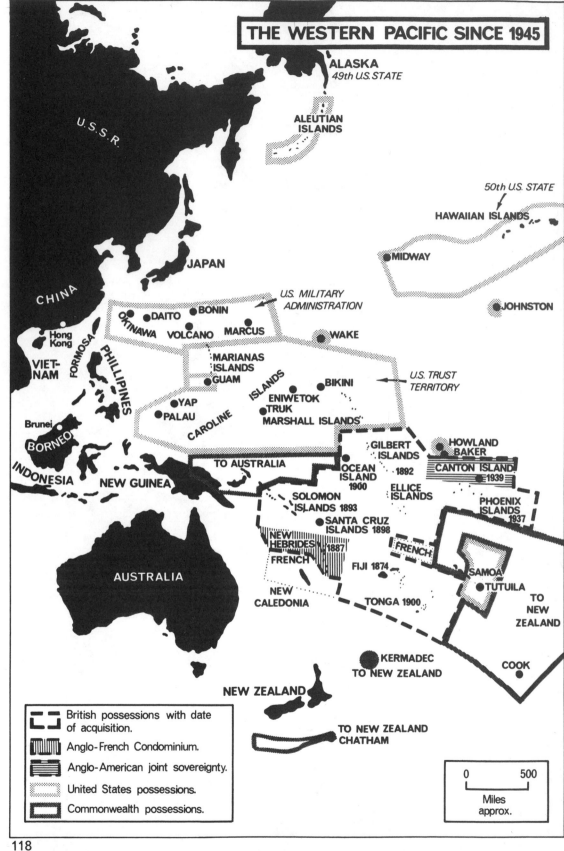

THE WESTERN PACIFIC SINCE 1945

ALASKA
49th U.S. STATE

ALEUTIAN
ISLANDS

50th U.S. STATE

HAWAIIAN ISLANDS

U.S.S.R.

MIDWAY

JOHNSTON

JAPAN

CHINA

Hong
Kong

FORMOSA

VIET-
NAM

PHILLIPINES

U.S. MILITARY
ADMINISTRATION

DAITO   BONIN

OKINAWA   VOLCANO   MARCUS

WAKE

MARIANAS
ISLANDS

GUAM

ISLANDS

BIKINI

U.S. TRUST
TERRITORY

YAP

PALAU

CAROLINE

ENIWETOK
TRUK

MARSHALL ISLANDS

Brunei

BORNEO

INDONESIA

NEW GUINEA

TO AUSTRALIA

OCEAN
ISLAND
1900

GILBERT
ISLANDS

1892

ELLICE
ISLANDS

HOWLAND
BAKER

CANTON ISLAND

1939

SOLOMON
ISLANDS 1893

SANTA CRUZ
ISLANDS 1898

PHOENIX
ISLANDS
1937

AUSTRALIA

NEW
HEBRIDES   1887
FRENCH

FIJI 1874

FRENCH

SAMOA

TUTUILA

TO
NEW
ZEALAND

NEW
CALEDONIA

TONGA 1900

KERMADEC
TO NEW ZEALAND

COOK

NEW ZEALAND

TO NEW ZEALAND
CHATHAM

British possessions with date
of acquisition.

Anglo-French Condominium.

Anglo-American joint sovereignty.

United States possessions.

Commonwealth possessions.

0   500

Miles
approx.

118